HIMALAYAN
DESERT

HIMALAYAN
DESERT

NINA RAO

Lustre Press
·
Roli Books

ISBN: 978-81-7436-413-5

© **Roli & Janssen BV 2007**
Published in India by
Roli Books in arrangement
with Roli & Janssen BV
M-75, G.K. II Market
New Delhi-110 048, India.
Phone: ++91-11-29212271,
29212782 Fax: 29217185
Email: roli@vsnl.com
Website: rolibooks.com

Printed and bound
in Singapore

PRECEDING PAGE 1: THE
SIXTEENTH CENTURY DHANKAR
GOMPA IN SPITI.

PRECEDING PAGES 2-3:
CHIU *GOMPA* AND ITS THREE
CHORTENS ARE SEEN ACROSS
THE TIBETAN PLATEAU NEAR
THE SACRED MOUNT KAILASH.
BOTH BUDDHIST AND HINDU
PILGRIMS VISIT THE SITE
LOCATED IN CHINA.

A YOUNG LADAKHI WOMAN
WEARING THE TRADITIONAL
ORNAMENTAL HEAD DRESS -
PERAK. A GOOD *PERAK* IS A
TREASURED HEIRLOOM
HANDED DOWN FROM MOTHER
TO DAUGHTER. THE *PERAK* IS
SHAPED LIKE THE HOODED
COBRA WITH ITS HEAD POISED
TO STRIKE. IT IS WORN OVER
THE FOREHEAD AND DOWN
THE BACK.

CONTENTS

JAMMU
AND
KASHMIR

INDUS

KARGIL
MULBEKH
ALCHI
LAMAYURU

LADAKH

SHYOK

KARAKORAM

SALT LAKE

LEH
SHEY
STOK
THIKSE

ZANSKAR

RANGE

MARAU

ZANSKAR
KARSHA GOMPA
PADUM
THONDE

ZANGLA

ZANSKAR

MOUNTAINS

Taglang Pass

INDUS

PANGONG TSO

CHENAB

RUPSHU

KURZOK

LAHUL
& SPITI
DARCHA
Bara Lacha Pass

TSO MORIRI

KAILAS

RAVI

KEYLONG

LOSAR

6

Hamta Jot Pass

SPITI

CHT

HIMACHAL PRADESH

KINNAUR

GOVIND
SAGAR

SATLUJ

PUNJAB

RAKAS LAKE

CHANDIGARH

BHAGIRATHI

ALAKNANDA

UTTAR
PRADESH

KALI

HARYANA

YAMUNA

RAMGANGA

SETI

INDIA

GANGA

DELHI

NE

N A

ET

RANGE

PHOKSUMDO LAKE

DOLPA   MUSTANG

oDUNAI

A *DROK PA* OR DARD VILLAGER FROM LADAKH. ORIGINALLY FROM THE GILGIT AREA OF JAMMU AND KASHMIR (NOW IN PAKISTAN), THE *DROK PA* SETTLED ALONG THE INDUS VALLEY, ADOPTED ISLAM AND INTRODUCED IRRIGATION IN THE REGION.

LEFT: MAP DEPICTING THE EXTENT OF THE AREA COVERED BY THE HIMALAYAN DESERT.

FOLLOWING PAGES 8-9: A NOVICE STANDS AT THE DOOR OF A MONASTERY IN MUSTANG, NEPAL. THIS STARK AND BARREN AREA HOLDS THE LAST REMNANTS OF TRUE TIBETAN LIFESTYLE UNTAINTED BY FOREIGN OCCUPATION. TO AVOID THIS UNIQUE KINGDOM BEING OVERRUN BY TOURISM THE REGION HAS BEEN GAZETTED AS A RESTRICTED AREA WITH ONLY SMALL NUMBERS OF TOURISTS GIVEN ACCESS EVERY YEAR.

PRECARIOUSLY
BALANCED AT THE
EDGE OF A CLIFF
IS THE PHUGTAL
MONASTERY IN
ZANSKAR. THIS
ELEVENTH CENTURY
GOMPA HAS BEEN
CARVED OUT OF THE
MOUNTAIN AND IS
HOME TO SOME
FIFTY MONKS.

FOLLOWING PAGE 12:
TOURISTS TREK ON
THE FROZEN ZANSKAR
RIVER, TRADITIONALLY
CALLED *CHADAR*, IN
LADAKH.

The Land of Citadels and Fortified Monasteries

T
he Himalaya is a vibrant, personal experience that is recaptured and renewed with every visit. Due to its immense height and massive topography, it creates a rain shadow zone to the west. Called the Great Himalayan Desert, this rain shadow zone extends from the Tibetan plateau and includes the Indian districts of Ladakh, Lahul, Kinnaur and Spiti as well as the enclave of Mustang in western Nepal. This vast desert is made up of barren rock and sand-covered valleys.

Though the Himalaya forms a gigantic east-west arc, dividing the Indian sub-continent from the high plateau of Central Asia, the Himalayan desert was not intended as a barrier between the lands which have given the world some of the greatest civilizations. In fact, its high passes facilitated an exchange of cultural ideas and traditions. Greek aesthetics merged with ideas from the Indian kingdoms and a local school of art developed. Persian, Indian and Greek cultures encountered each other at what today is known as the Karakoram Highway, linking the sub-continent to Kashgar and Khotan, the southern-most market towns on the ancient silk route.

Tossing in the turbulence of this cold and arid land, caught in the current of a powerful and exacting habitat, responding to the tug of time to shape their lives, the people of this desert have lived out their

AN AERIAL VIEW OF THE CITY OF LEH,
AN HISTORICAL ENTREPOT AND AN
IMPORTANT MARKET.

dreams in a sacred agreement with the elements. The mountains for these people are homes of gods and goddesses who possess supernatural powers of defence. They are not to be torn apart, walked over or climbed upon; they are the sacred land where the living and the dead walk hand in hand, not an arena for sport and adventure.

The ecological prudence and restraint shown by the nomadic wanderers in their pattern of transhumance is till today a guide for all those who wish to learn about the great Himalayan desert. They have moved up and down the mountain slopes, conserving resources for the long term, even though such restrictions have made their immediate present difficult. Vegetation has been nurtured by animal dung, pastures have been visited by seasonal rotation, communal resources have been shared justly, taboos have been respected because they represent the wisdom of the elders, and the life-cycle of the animal and human resource-base has been protected to ensure sustainability for future generations.

To an outsider, the Himalayan desert is a wild, desolate and little known region; it is a land of great peaks and deep valleys; of precipitous gorges cut by persistent rivers that rise in the high plateau of snow and ice; a barren and beautiful land of intense sunlight, clear

THE TABO MONASTERY IN SPITI STANDS ON THE BARREN, ARID, SNOW COVERED ROCKY DESERT OF THE TABO VALLEY AT A HEIGHT OF 3050 METRES. THE MONASTERY HAS PRESERVED THE GLORIOUS HERITAGE, TRADITIONS AND CULTURE OF BUDDHISM THROUGH THE PASSAGE OF CENTURIES.

COLD AND FORBIDDING YET ATTRACTIVE BECAUSE IT IS RARELY VISITED, THE NORTH RIMO GLACIER IN LADAKH. DUE TO ITS REMOTE LOCATION IN THE HEART OF THE EASTERN KARAKORAM, RIMO WAS LITTLE-KNOWN AND ALMOST ENTIRELY UNVISITED UNTIL THE TWENTIETH CENTURY. *FOLLOWING PAGES 20-21:* IT IS HARD TO BELIEVE THAT THESE STRANGELY CONTOURED, CRAGGY OUTCROPS ARE ACTUALLY BADLANDS NEAR LAMAYURU MONASTERY, NEAR LEH IN LADAKH.

sparkling air and wonderful colours. Here, both man and mountain seem to have been fashioned from the same earth and seem to share something in common. In a world that is mapped in the minds of the wandering nomads, it is only the hardy races which can cope with the wearisome life that demands hardship and struggle to survive.

Political whirlwinds have often accompanied the sandstorms at these heights. Religion, art and culture have flourished despite the antagonism between the nomadic herdsmen, hunters and agriculturists. Water—the wealth of the desert—has determined the way of life of these people and overshadowed their relationships right up to the recent past.

Popularly known as the crossroads of the world, it is here in the high reaches of the Himalayan desert that the settled people tamed their wild conquerors. These civilized races often had to escape or start afresh in entirely new areas, when their civilizational advantage was not to the taste of the invaders. In times of peace, city-states grew in size and prosperity, embellished with fine mansions, palaces, monasteries, mosques and markets. Artists and craftsmen developed their skills to establish their own canons. Scholars and merchants travelled from court to court enriching the trade routes from east to west. Hospitality to strangers, who were the source of new ideas and influences, became a tradition for a people sophisticated enough to want to increase their knowledge. Merchants were also welcomed as a respite from the ceaseless toil of subsistence farming.

This vast area has individual features that are extremely complex and no single feature can be considered representative of the region. The inordinate complexity of the formational process is indicated by the unnatural order of the various ranges, the flatness of the river beds and the incisive gorges that seek an opening into the plains. These form several divisions based on the drainage areas of the four major river systems: the Indus, known as the *Sing ka bab* (Rising from the Lion's Mouth) in the west, the Bhramaputra or the *Ster-chuk ka bab* (Rising from the Horse's Mouth) in the east, the Ganges, called the *Mab cha ka bab* (Rising from the Peacock's Mouth) in the north and the Sutlej, *Lang-chin ka bab* (Rising from the Mouth of the Elephant) to the south. The tendency to personify rivers and to give them human expressions and emotions was perhaps an attempt by the locals, Tibetans and Hindus, to bring them under control.

The greater part of the 8,000 meter high Himalaya lies above the snow line. This is the home of the snowfields that feed the glaciers and the torrential streams that tumble down steep gradients to the plains below. The rugged landscape and the high peaks are the result of fluvial erosion. The great glaciers include the Siachen (70 km), the Baltoro (60 km), the Biafo (60 km) and the Hispar (62 km). Found in the Karakoram range, they feed the Nubra and Shyok rivers that form the lifeline for these hidden valleys, that are otherwise unconnected by road. In fact, this region saw no intervention from the outside world until the armies of India, China and Pakistan turned Ladakh into the

THE ZANGLA *GOMPA* STANDS ALONE AND REMOTE IN ZANGLA, ONE OF THE MOST FORBIDDING AREAS IN THE HIMALAYA.

FACING PAGE: THE KARAKORAM RANGE SWEEPS ACROSS THE NORTHERN BORDER OF LADAKH.

FOLLOWING PAGE 24-25: A *CHORTEN* WITH HORSE MOTIF OUTSIDE TEGAR *GOMPA*, IN THE NUBRA VALLEY OF LADAKH.

highest battleground in the world. High altitude lakes have also been formed by glacial depressions and rock falls, for example, the Pangong and Tso Morari in the Rupshu region.

Ladakh, a land of many names, like *Maryul* (Lowland), *Khachanpa* (the Land of Snow) and *Ladwag* (Ladakhi name for the region) is situated between the Karakoram and Pangong ranges. It is India's highest plateau, containing the remains of three peneplains at heights between 5,300 to 5,800 meters that are mostly above the snow line. Its height is one of the reasons for the dry and desert-like conditions. The plateau is dissected into the Lingzi Tang plain, the Lokzhung plain, the Aksai Chin and the Soda, all of them so dry and bare that even nomads do not venture into this terrain. Similarly, the Chandra valley of Lahul is uninhabited, except for nomadic shepherds in search of pastures on the southern slopes.

The Himalaya to the north and its spurs to the north-east constitute two closed sides of a box. The monsoon currents cannot enter this region and the extreme difference in day and night temperatures shatters rocks and creates fissures in the hardest surfaces. Rock and ice falls are common occurrences which threaten existence.

All along this vast region there are remains of flourishing human settlements with irrigation works, forests and evidence of a more moist climate. The continental desiccation has been exacerbated through increasing aridity caused by the deflection of moisture bearing winds along the northern slopes and the disruption of drainage lines along the river basins.

The high plateau receives only 3 cm of rain annually. Cultivable land is not easy to find. The population is sparse, 2 persons per sq km, and communications are difficult. The presence of armies have brought in roads and technology which have had an impact on these frontier regions in more than one sense.

However, language, lifestyle and the customs of the people vary from one valley to the next. Stock breeding, particularly of the hardy yaks, goral sheep and goats, has been the primary resource of these mountain communities, supplemented by trade in the winter when there are no pastures to seek.

Travellers in this desert have described the illusory sounds and mirages that have lured the unwary to

death. These are usually the tramp and hum of the caravans and at other times, the sound of a variety of musical instruments, particularly the drum. The shepherds, porters and traders have described these as the work of evil spirits or the voices of their ancestors calling to them.

The resource base of the Himalayan desert is highly diverse and heterogeneous, added to which are spatial discontinuities caused by altitude, slope and relief. Historical, cultural and ethnic specificities have introduced further dimensions to the naturally determined constraints of the mountains. Indigenous institutions, knowledge systems and traditional survival strategies are a part of the mountain perspective that are not valued adequately in the march towards modernisation. Just as the Moravian missions replaced Tibetan medicine and lamaism with allopathy and western education, the same modernising intervention through development in these marginalised regions has created conflicts with the environment and amongst the communities.

Caravans through history have only skirted the edges of this fabled land. Although the area is vast, few roads pass through it and life has revolved around a few settlements that are nurtured by natural water courses, wherever they exist. The north-south movement is restricted to a few icy passes which have their own grim tales for the traveller. Dangerously narrow, at a height of over 5,000 meters with precipitous drops into deep ravines, they are the most difficult to cross.

While Buddhism survives along the intricate network of rivers that feed the Indus, the Sutlej and the Chenab, the trading importance of Ladakh and its environs has been replaced by its strategic importance. It is clear that despite its isolation, this region has had a turbulent history reflected in its mixed racial stock: Chinese, Tibetan, Kashmiri and Indo-Iranian (Dardic). In the first century AD, the extent of the Kushan empire—a Buddhist people descended from the Yueh-Chih, a Mongolian tribe—created a stable and prosperous basis for long distance trade. To their west, the Parthians were not so free and open, being middlemen in the trade with Rome. To the east lay China, across the Taklamakan desert. Some oasis kingdoms of the Tarim Basin like Khotan, Yarkhand and Kashgar were more friendly with the Kushans than with the Chinese. The Kushans converted their neighbours to Buddhism instead of exacting tribute. Shrines and temples became the mainstay of the traders on the silk route and later for the pilgrims. When Fa-hsien visited Khotan in the fourth century, he found a world at peace, with richly decorated monasteries and no sign of devastation by the Mongolian hordes. Hsuang-tsang describes the now vanished Sogdians as the guardians of the trade routes. They were peaceable and industrious and divided their time between farming and trade. They were also noted artisans renowned for wood carving,

FACING PAGE: THE GIANT FIFTEEN METER HIGH IMAGE OF THE MAITREYA BUDDHA DOMINATES THE THIKSE MONASTERY OUTSIDE LEH.

glass making, carpet weaving and metal works, crafts which are still practised in the high desert.

The history of Spiti has been closely linked to that of Ladakh until it was brought under the administration of Kullu by the British to access the shawl wool trade of the Chang Thang plateau. Lahul continued to be a part of the kingdom of Gu-je until the seventeenth century when it was transferred to Chamba, and subsequently to the Sikh kingdom that took over Chamba. The nomadic life (*chang pa*) is a remnant of the old lifestyle of the Ladakhi and Spiti people, similar to the Chiangs who used to roam the pastures of Central Asia. Till today, the farmers and dairy producers continue their barter economy. This division is climatic and so ingrained that neither Buddhism nor feudalism has interrupted the chain of production in the region.

Between the seventh and ninth centuries, Islam made inroads into the Himalayan desert through an alliance between the Western Turks and Tibetans against the Chinese. Invasions from Baltistan, (now in the northern frontier region of Pakistan) converted the populations of Kashmir and Nubra. The Arabs were to prove implacable enemies of Buddhism and the Tibetan way of life. Twentieth century archaeologists have found that the dry desert sands have preserved deserted Buddhist centres almost intact on the silk route between India and China.

THE SPECTACULAR SILT FORMATIONS ON THE PEAKS IN LADAKH.

LADAKH IS SITUATED BETWEEN THE KARAKORAM AND PANGONG RANGES. HERE THE SNOW-COVERED HIMALAYAN RANGES CAN BE SEEN IN THEIR MORNING GLORY.

FACING PAGE: THE RIDZONG *GOMPA* APPEARS SUDDENLY AT THE END OF A WINDING WALK THROUGH THE VALLEY ON THE ROAD TO LADAKH.

The accommodation between Islam and Buddhism continued till recent times; Ladakhi kings often took Balti princesses as wives or themselves converted to Islam. Marriage between Buddhist women and Muslim men was not questioned and the mixed community of Argun families was an interesting feature in the land of the lamas. More recently, in the wake of militancy in the Kashmir valley, the two communities have once again begun to view each other with hostility. The mistrust could partly be due to the control of tourism by the Kashmiris as well as their domination of Ladakhi administration. Kashmir is considered an alien power. The movement for an autonomous hill council, which was successfully established in 1993, has helped to a limited extent to overcome the schism.

In the thirteenth century, the Mongols began to migrate from Manchuria and brought in new racial characteristics. They had round heads, pale skins, slanted eyes and high cheek-bones. They were not hirsute and had so much value for water that they were known to be malodorous, not bathing for days together. These characteristics are shared by the desert people even today.

Genghis Khan, Kublai Khan and Tamurlane established the military as well as the cultural excellence of the extensive Mongolian empire, with Samarkhand as the greatest city of the fifteenth century. Babur, a descendent of Genghis Khan, conquered India in the sixteenth century after he was ousted from Ferghana and founded the Mughal dynasty. As Russia and China expanded, the freedom of the nomads was curtailed and they were confined to the high valleys of the Himalaya. By the nineteenth century, India was under the control of the British East India Company and the great game of spying between Russia and Britain brought many travellers to the desert domain.

What had once been the preserve of monks, merchants, peasants, and shepherds was now mapped by members of geographical societies, scientists, botanists and tea traders, all of whom carried surveying material. Native 'pundits' were sent by the Survey of India disguised as holy men and pilgrims because of the local people's hostility to white men. These early explorers made headlines in their home countries, and travellers were attracted to explore the Himalayan desert for themselves. However, many of the treasures of the lost cities and monasteries that were excavated in the twentieth century were carried away to Europe. Ladakh has suffered in the same way ever since it was opened to tourism in 1974.

Even after the Independence of India in 1947, the Himalayan desert has remained a battleground. No longer do caravans trace their lengthy routes across the high passes as various tribesmen fight over territory and resources. Today, regular air services link Ladakh with the rest of the country. Helicopter services access the remotest areas of the districts above the snow line. The Border Roads Organisation maintains the roads and the army has established an all-season road via Manali, which has proved to be a popular entry point for tourists. Regular bus services connect all the districts to the capital of Himachal Pradesh, Shimla. Satellite communication has brought television and telephone to the major settlements, integrating them into the mainstream of Indian social and political life. Projects like the Igufey canal and social forestry have helped to push the desert further away from the settlements. The presence of the army and civil works by the administration have undermined the control of the feudal families. These families had supported the monasteries (*gompas*), not only in terms of land and money, but also by sponsoring novice lamas. These changes have brought about a transformation in terms of language, manners, values and attire. The younger generation is no longer enthusiastic about monasticism. It prefers employment in the army, contracting for development projects or providing services and facilities for tourists. The era of independence and self-sufficiency of Ladakh and its neighbouring areas has come to a close. Traditional ties which fertilised the religion, art and culture of the region have been abruptly arrested by boundaries which are contested till today. A fiercely independent people have been declared tribal and have become dependent on the developmental agencies of the central government as they try to enter the mainstream of modern Indian life.

FACING PAGE: PERCHED HIGH ON AN OVERHANG IS THE SIXTEENTH CENTURY DHANKAR *GOMPA*. ONCE A PRISON IT NOW HOUSES OVER 150 LAMAS AND CONTAINS BUDDHIST SCRIPTURES AND MURALS OF HEALING BUDDHAS.

THE ANCIENT TIBETAN KINGDOM OF GU-JE INCLUDED LAHUL
UNTIL THE SEVENTEENTH CENTURY. A SPECTACULAR VIEW
OF THE MOUNTAINS IN THOLING IN GU-JE.

FACING PAGE: WILLOWS AND POPLARS BRING THE BEAUTY OF
AUTUMN COLOURS TO THE BARE LADAKHI LANDSCAPE.

Yet, the desert retains its character. It remains remote, sparsely populated, close to its religious traditions. With outside influences beginning to undermine its society and culture, documentation of people's art and architectural heritage, oral, literary and folk traditions is being given importance. Ecology and environment are being protected by several non-governmental organisations, many of which are headed and controlled by local people. Traditional beliefs and practices, so closely linked to Buddhism, are also being protected and revived.

The recent changes have not transformed the basic simplicity of life in the Himalayan desert. Changes have come, but the classical lifestyle has proved successful beyond doubt. It has maintained its chronological seam in relating to nature, reality and daily life and the vehicle to communicate it to others. This is what conveys to the visitor a sense of its pride, self-sufficiency and its rock solid foundation. The weaknesses and transgressions are a part of the desert's charm. It creates in us the modest desire to share in the people's dreams, to be a part of their longings, to respond to their imagination, not in the form of amicable condescension but as an enabling participant in the cross-current of life.

LAMAYURU, ON THE LEH-SRINAGAR ROAD, IS LADAKH'S OLDEST LIVING MONASTERY. IT IS ALSO A REGION THAT HAS THE MOST INTERESTING MORAIN FORMATIONS THAT ARE TYPICAL OF THE HIMALAYAN DESERT. IN THE FOREGROUND ARE THE *CHORTENS*. THE VILLAGE STRAGGLES DOWN THE SLOPE, REFLECTING THE POSITION OF THE MONASTERY IN THE SOCIAL HIERARCHY.

FOLLOWING PAGE 38: THE IMAGE OF THE MAITREYA IS IN THE CENTRE OF THE TEMPLE TO ALLOW TWO ROWS OF MONKS TO RECITE THE SCRIPTURES. THE CANONICAL LIBRARY IS SITUATED BEHIND THE IMAGE IN THE *DU KHANG* (TEMPLE).

Trans Himalaya: The Tibetan Empire

The main range or the Great Himalaya—known in ancient literature as Himgiri—rises like a massive screen south of the 5,000 meter high plateau of Tibet. This is the region known as the Trans Himalaya, an ill-defined mountain tract covering an area of 1,000 km. There are no deep river gorges here, but it is home to some of the highest passes and the sources of the Bhramaputra, Indus and Sutlej rivers, as well as the Kailash Range. This is also the land of fluttering prayer flags invoking the favour of the lord of compassion. The famous *kumbum* (a stupa containing thousands of images and multiple chapels) at Gyantse represents the importance of Buddhism in giving courage to the faithful as they perform the *parikrama* (ritual circumambulation) of the stupa.

The other mountain range in Tibet is the great Karakoram, known in Sanskrit literature as Krishnagiri, and as the Black Gravel mountains to the travellers on the silk route. It lies north of the Indus, in a steppe-like, semi-desert landscape. The Great Asian Desert, with the Thar in the south and the Taklamakan in the north, incorporates the Himalayan rain shadow zone.

The Tibetan plateau, the unique site of a sophisticated medieval culture, is reached after great physical hardship, crossing wide valleys, undulating sand dunes and small villages. The esoteric world of

THE MONKS AND LAMAS CONDUCT THE FESTIVAL AT DERGE GONCHEN MONASTERY IN TIBET. THIS RECENTLY RENOVATED *GOMPA* IS THE SEAT OF THE SAKYA TRIZIN, HEAD OF THE SAKYA-PA SCHOOL.

KHAM OR EASTERN
TIBET CONTAINS
SOME OF THE MOST
RUGGED MOUNTAINS
AND DEEP GORGES.
THIS FERTILE LAND,
THE MOST
POPULATED REGION
IN TIBET, IS NOW A
PART OF CHINESE
TERRITORY.

FACING PAGE:
A BON-PO
MONASTERY IN
THE WESTERN
TIBETAN KINGDOM
OF GU-JE.

lamas has remained isolated and closed, as much due to the geographical and climatic conditions as due to the desire to remain true to its religious beliefs.

Tibet and the Tarim Basin are the most desolate reminders of an on-going historical process, to which human intervention and pressures are adding their own stress. As rivers have disappeared into the growing volumes of sand or when precipitation was low due to climatic changes, the desert spread itself.

The landscape of the Tibetan plateau is barren as patches of vegetation and settlements grow further apart. Since the Chinese takeover, there is a new route to Tibet across the Lakpa and Tsu passes. This takes one to Zhigatse, the old capital of Tibet and the home of the Tashilumpo monastery, founded by the first Panchen Lama (teacher of the Dalai Lama) in 1477. Built on a sacred burial site, it has the tallest gilded copper image of the Buddha Maitreya. The monastery is testimony to the fact that Zhigatse was the gateway to the later Buddhist kingdoms.

THE HIGH DESERT
NEAR THOLING, THE
CAPITAL OF THE
ANCIENT KINGDOM
OF GU-JE. WITH ITS
SPECTACULAR VIEWS,
THOLING GIVES ONE
A REAL SENSE OF
TIBET AS THE ROOF
OF THE WORLD.

Buddhism transformed the various tribes and autonomous clans into centralised kingdoms, thus encouraging the development of feudalism in the Himalayan region bordering Tibet. The role that the Buddhist kings played in subduing the tribes, collectively called the followers of the Bon religion, can be seen in the history of Tibet. The expansion of the Kingdom of Lhasa corresponded to the spread of Buddhism. The western Tibetan kingdom of Gu-je (which included parts of Ladakh, Lahul, Spiti and Kinnaur) covered the area from Tholing to the borders of Kashmir, the forts and monasteries being evidence of its imperial control. The subjugation of the clans was violent and force was the basis of territorial control. The concept of the fortress-monastery was a product of this time: realising the need of the people, the monasteries emerged as politico-religious organisations that provided defence and administration along with spiritual guidance.

The Bhotias, an ethnic Tibetan community who migrated from the inhospitable plateau, are found in the border lands of India and Nepal. As they moved, they carried with them the prayer flag, the prayer wheel and the *chorten* (reliquary object), a vital part of daily life in the deserts, thus spreading the religion.

After the death of the Buddha, three schools of Buddhism emerged: Mahayana, Hinayana and Vajrayana. It was the Mahayana form that triumphed in Tibet and its surrounding areas since it was a socially more relevant philosophy. Apart from caring for its monks and novices, Mahayana Buddhism established

effective contact with the community. Also, since the new sect wanted to gather adherents, it adopted a doctrine which allowed space for secular life.

During the reign of the Kushan king, Kanishka, the Mahayana school turned militant; the emperor took the title of Dharmapala, the defender of faith. In Tibet, this militancy led to the splitting of the Buddhists into four major sects: *Nying-ma-pa* (the elders), *Ka-dam-pa* (black hat), *Drug-pa* (red hat) and *Ge-lug-pa* (yellow hat), a process in which monks fought each other. Kye monastery in Spiti has a fine collection of weapons used by the monks at the time.

Despite the political and religious turmoil, travelogues show that traffic through this torturous land was fairly routine. Guidebooks listed the kind of goods that were desired, market towns where stopovers could be made and supplies replenished and the best areas to pick up new ideas, products and technologies. Travellers were attracted by the sheer pleasure and the adventures that the Himalayan highway offered.

A journey through the great Tibetan desert was one of great length and hardship. Food and water to last several months had to be carried for both man and beast. Besides, there were the vagaries of weather, unfriendly lands and people, strange languages, and the eternal fear of failure or death. The dangers of thirst, cold, sandstorm, snow blizzard and animal attack were constant. But there were compensations: the invigoration of ascent and the arrival at the threshold of a high valley; the clear water of a

A YOUNG MONK ROTATING A PRAYER WHEEL ALSO CALLED MANI WHEELS BY TIBETANS. A PRAYER WHEEL IS A WHEEL ON A SPINDLE ON WHICH PRAYERS OR MANTRAS ARE WRITTEN. ACCORDING TO TIBETAN BUDDHISTS SPINNING PRAYER WHEELS HAS THE SAME EFFECT AS ORALLY RECITING PRAYERS.

mountain stream; the flight of water birds or the sudden appearance of a herd of wild asses; the welcome sight of a nomadic camp or a fortified town with its guardian *gompa*. The simple comforts of these monasteries were like undreamed of luxuries. Even when sea routes were discovered by adventurers, the overland route was not forgotten. It continued to be a busy thoroughfare for the towns established by conquerors, nourished by colonists and refugees, enriched by traders, edified by lamas and pilgrims. They continued to grow even as the sands claimed some of them in the course of time.

As Freya Stark wrote in *Rome on the Euphrates: The Story of a Frontier*, 'no mere river of water can be compared to this perennial stream of caravans, that has carried a half of human history, from stage to stage, from wasteland to wasteland and climate to climate, on the puny strength of men.'

The most sacred Buddhist shrine in the Tibetan plateau is the Jokhang temple at Lhasa. It is a part of the legacy of strong cultural links between Vajrayana Buddhism of Tibet, faithful to its Indian inspiration, and the institution of the *gompa* which was basic to its growth. Songsen Gampo of Tibet was the first king to exploit the power of Buddhism in the seventh century when his Nepalese queen, Bhrikuti, built the temple on a site divined by his Chinese wife, Wengcheng, as the power centre of Tibet. She herself built the Ramoche temple at a site that she, as a clairvoyant, said was the location of the subterranean crystal palace of the Nagas (gods of the nether world). Mahayana Buddhism crossed over the bridge to Central Asia, Tibet and China on the strength of the vast number of *sutras* and *tantras*, canonical works that needed to be housed, indexed and referred to. Thus, the monastery became the centre of scholarship. Once the mission of spreading the word had been accomplished, Buddhism became a powerful contemplative force.

TWO NOMADS AND THEIR CAMEL CARAVAN
WITH OTHER ANIMALS WALK ALONG A ROAD
ACROSS A DESERT FROM KARGHALIK
TO TIBET.

NOMADS IN EASTERN TIBET WITH HERBAL APHRODISIACS. TIBETAN MEDICINE IS ONE OF THE OLDEST FORMS IN THE WORLD. IT UTILIZES UP TO 2,000 TYPES OF PLANTS, 40 ANIMAL SPECIES, AND 50 MINERALS.

FOLLOWING PAGE 52: THE PICTURESQUE ROUTE TO MOUNT KAILASH AND LAKE MANASAROVAR. MOUNT KAILASH HAS THE UNIQUE DISTINCTION OF BEING SACRED TO FOUR RELIGIONS AND IS VISITED BY THOUSANDS EACH YEAR. THE JOURNEY REQUIRES WEEKS OF DIFFICULT OFTEN DANGEROUS TRAVEL.

Ladakh
Lahul
Spiti And
Kinnaur

L adakh is for the most part a desert of bare crags and granite dust, with arid table-lands, no forests and few pastures. But braving this cold and inhospitable nature are settlements at an elevation of 12,000 to 16,000 ft. Ladakhi texts testify to the slow emergence of the Ladakhi plateau from the sea in the pre-Cambrian period and the consequent desiccation of the area as the Himalaya continued to grow. Early records substantiate the difficulties of travel, the major movement being those of Kashmiri merchants and local traders who monopolised the emporium trade.

Ladakh's historical records go back to 400 BC when Sargyal established the kingdoms of Ladakh and Tibet. *Gyalpo* or hereditary kingship was established in 333 AD, replacing the earlier feudal clans. The Lha-chen dynasty ruled Ladakh until the coming of the Mughals. It was in this period that the famous Buddhist text, the *Kanjur,* was written. Gyalpo Rinchin of this dynasty became the ruler of Kashmir (1324-27 AD) and was influenced by the Sufi saints who converted him to Islam. In 1531, Ladakh was invaded by Mirza Haidar Daulat, an adventurer from Central Asia.

In 1541, Daulat Mirza was invited by Kashmiri nobles to attack Kashmir again. He provided the route to the conquest of Ladakh, but the severe cold of Tibet defeated him as it defeated others like Zorawar Singh, the general of the Dogras, who ruled Kashmir between the

MANE WALLS AND *CHORTENS* IN ZANSKAR INSPIRE TREKKERS AND TRADERS TO REACH THEIR DESTINATION.

sixteenth and twentieth centuries. Ladakh thus was a stepping stone to the conquest of Kashmir and Tibet. Its prosperity was related to its role as a provision station between Khotan and Kashmir. Adventurers knew that the monasteries were repositories of treasures collected over the years. At Hemis, one can see the strong room where the gold and silver are still stored. The room is built into the rock and difficult to identify.

The Namgyal dynasty was established in the sixteenth century, with its capital at Leh. Sovang Namgyal extended this kingdom to the outskirts of Lhasa in the east and Shigar, Kharko and Baltistan in the north, forcing the rulers of these states to become his

CLOUDS DESCENDING ON THE SACRED PEAKS OF KINNAUR, RENOWNED FOR THE KINNER KAILASH YATRA.

FACING PAGE: THE 17,200 FEET HIGH NYERTSE-LA PASS SOUTH OF LAMAYURU IN LADAKH.

FOLLOWING PAGES: ALSO KNOWN AS 'LITTLE TIBET' SPITI IS HOME TO SOME OF THE OLDEST BUDDHIST MONASTERIES AND TEMPLES IN THE WORLD INCLUDING THE FOURTEENTH CENTURY KYE MONASTERY.

vassals. Sovang was a great builder too; he built a great palace on Tsemo Hill which has now perished. But the temple decorated with Buddhist images still survives and is worth a visit as it has a panoramic view of the valley. One can almost share the feeling of the temple guardians as they look down upon the town. Sovang

LADAKH IS HOME TO A NUMBER OF ENDANGERED SPECIES INCLUDING THE TIBETAN WILD ASS ALSO KNOWN AS KIANG. THE WILD ASS IS FOUND ONLY IN TWO PLACES IN INDIA - IN HIGH PLATEAUS (5,000 M) OF LADAKH AND IN NORTH SIKKIM ALONG THE INDO-TIBET BORDER.

FACING PAGE: DOUBLE-HUMPED BACTRAIN CAMELS IN NUBRA, LADAKH.

Namgyal also built roads and bridges across the rivers of Ladakh. He was succeeded by his brother Jamyang who was defeated by the chief of Skardu (in present Pakistan), Raja Ali Sher. Jamyang and Ali Sher made a matrimonial alliance by marriage with each other's daughters. The Skardu princess Argiyal Khatun gave birth to two sons, Singe and Norbu.

Singe (lion) Namgyal ascended the throne in 1610. He subdued Purang, Zanskar and Spiti and defeated the Raja of Baltistan who attempted to reconquer Ladakh. He tried to annex Tibet, but was unsuccessful. He was subdued by the Mughal army which came from Kashmir. Like all Ladakhi *gyalpos*, Singe's primary concern was to somehow buy peace with Kashmir and China so that Ladakh could prosper. Singe was also a devout Buddhist and he established the *gompas* or monasteries of Hemis, Chimre, Hanle and Timosgang. His campaigns across the valleys of Ladakh have enriched them with *mane* walls (stone walls on which travellers and pilgrims inscribe the Buddhist *mantra* or chant *Om Mani Padma Om*).

Singe's son Delden was a benevolent and popular ruler. The Rengmo *mane* wall leading to Leh was built by him. He also built the Shey palace and monastery which are still a major attraction for visitors. Once the Ladakhi army was defeated at Bodh Kharbu near Kargil and the Mughals invaded Ladakh, Delden submitted to the mighty Muslim power. He built the famous mosque in Leh bazaar where he agreed to get the *khutba* recited in honour of the Mughal emperor Jahangir. In the reign of his son Delek, Tibet invaded Ladakh. He retreated to

Bazgo fort, and since the governor of Kashmir came to his aid, Delek took the name Aqbat Mehmood Khan and established a trade link between Kashmir and Tibet.

Once peace was established, the next king, Nyima became a great patron of art and letters. He established a paper mill and introduced hand-printing. Sacred Buddhist texts were edited and printed extensively during his reign. Many well-known foreigners visited his court at Leh and his palace at Nubra is still worth a visit. After his death in 1750, the subsequent Ladakhi kings were weak and ineffectual. Zorawar Singh, commander of the Dogra army, took advantage of the disorder to invade Ladakh in 1833. He entered over the Botkol pass between Kargil and Kishtwar, and defeated the Ladakhi army at Suru.

However, a large Ladakhi army awaited the Dogras at Mulbekh, so Zorawar made a strategic retreat to his fortress at Suru. After four months of skirmishes, the Ladakhi king appealed for peace and paid a large sum in exchange. Zorawar then proceeded to Lamayuru and subdued Zanskar. He built a fort at Leh which can be visited today, but in place of Zorawar Singh's garrison, we now have the Indian army. The mud fort is an attractive remnant of Ladakh's turbulent past. It is also a sad reminder of the end of the independent Kingdom of Ladakh, since it became a part of the state of Jammu and Kashmir by the treaty of Amritsar, signed by the British and the Dogras. Zorawar Singh invaded Baltistan and elated with his success, marched on to Tibet. He defeated

the Tibetan outpost at Rudok, but perished at the legendary battle of Kardamkhar.

Tibetan interest in Ladakh dates from the seventh century AD. It was at this time that Lalitaditya Muktapada, the king of Kashmir and a great patron of Buddhism, defeated the Dards, of Indo-Iranian stock similar to the Kashmiris and Tibetans. In the tenth and eleventh centuries, with the establishment of the kingdom of Gu-je, Ladakh began to integrate with Tibetan culture. Lahul was also a part of the kingdom of Gu-je and continued to pay tribute to Ladakh until it was annexed by the Sikhs, a martial community from the plains of Punjab, in 1840. It was invaded by the Tibetans in 1055, and by Kublai Khan's troops in 1262. By the seventeenth century, Spiti had come under the rule of Ladakh. The Balti penetration into Ladakh in 1740 extended to Spiti as did Zorawar Singh's invasion a century later. Spiti was coveted by the British for its access to Chang Thang, where the Pashmina herds were located. They traded Spiti with Kashmir and brought it under the administration of Kullu.

Coming back to Ladakh, though it is divided into three administrative divisions of Kargil, Zanskar and Leh, the geographical divisions are more important for the understanding of Ladakhi culture. Central Ladakh covers the villages along the Indus and the streams and rivers

FACING PAGE: THE ORACLE (*LA-BA*) AT MATHO MONASTERY IN LADAKH CUTTING HIS TONGUE. EVERY YEAR, DURING THE ANNUAL FESTIVAL IN MARCH, THE ORACLES ARE SAID TO BE POSSESSED BY SPIRITS WHEN THEY PERFORM DRAMATIC FEATS AND ALSO FORETELL THE FUTURE OF THE PEOPLE AND THE REGION.

that form its tributaries. This includes the extraordinarily fertile and picturesque region between Lamayuru and Leh, which forms the primary tourist circuit of Ladakh. In the early days, visitors who came along this road were amazed not only by the wealth of culture and hospitality of the people but also by the splendour of the Indus river which adds life and colour to the dun-coloured landscape. The winter route was via Kullu, since guides and porters refused to brave the passes on the road from Kashmir for fear of whirlwinds in the moraines. Even today, 80 ft high walls of ice and deep glacial depressions make the road difficult and dangerous. Army convoys have added to the delay through a gate system which controls up and down traffic. However, there is a sense of achievement as one drives over the Fotu-la pass on the Kashmir side or the Baralacha pass on the Kullu side. *Mane* walls and towers stand as reminders of those who managed to reach their destination safely, and give courage to those who come after them.

Exchanging wool for grain, the traffic between Ladakh and Lahul has been undeterred by the difficult terrain. The hardy, well-trained ponies and sheep which are used by the local communities for carrying goods have ensured that trade between these remote valleys has remained alive. Protected by amulets blessed by the lamas, these wandering communities have maintained their oral traditions, even though the fortified strongholds of the past have now been exchanged for peaceable commerce and interaction.

The old road to Ladakh can be seen from Darch across beds of snow, small patches of herbage and narrow streams escaping from beneath the snow fields. The path lies over slips of rock hemmed in by barren and high mountains which darken the narrow valley, with no villages or signs of life. At the Baralacha-la, *mane* stones and streamers maintain a lonely vigil over a plain which marks the remains of a mighty mountain destroyed in all probability by an earthquake. Crossing the pass, many have felt the effects of exposure and fatigue. The sun can be intensely hot while the piercing winds extremely cold. Sunburn and headaches are common discomforts. The plains below are barren, when not covered with sandstone rocks which are tinted yellow due to their iron content. Snow melt runs off rapidly at this height leaving the area dry. This is the Ling-ti plain that divides Lahul from Zanskar.

As the road zig-zags towards Zanskar, the mountains resembling towers, columns and spires—with caverns of great depth housing trickling streams of fine sand—are often mistaken for temples or monasteries. The black and slate coloured rocks make the area forbidding and it is a relief to reach the Rup-shu plateau and meet the caravans of traders, and perhaps catch a glimpse of wild sheep.

On crossing the Tung-lung, granite peaks pierce the skies once again. Here, one can see the snow clouds advance and retreat between the crests of the high summits. The shepherd station and the monastery at Giah must have given refuge to many a weary traveller.

PIN VALLEY, SPITI: IT IS THE WOMEN WHO WORK IN THE FIELDS IN THE HIGH DESERT, THE MEN BEING AWAY TRADING OR PASTURING THE ANIMALS.

At Giah, one can see the close relationship between administrative and religious power: the traditional feudal chief is attended by the *Kah lun* or headman and the two in turn accept the supremacy of the lama or Kushok. This is a pattern repeated all over the region, although feudal titles have been removed in the modern state. Lamas are not mere spiritual guides but serve as chief municipal officers of the towns. They have represented the Ladakh region in the Parliament as well as on the Minorities Commission. Some of them have even served as Indian ambassadors to Buddhist countries.

Coming back to Giah's geography, poplar plantations are the only sign of vegetation near the township. The river is bordered by rock walls studded with quartz and crystals. The road weaves back and forth across the river. At Upshi, the Giah river falls into the Yuma, the main branch of the Indus. This is a small township of stone houses, golden fields and the recently set up Pashmina goat station, where research is being conducted to improve the quality and output of the famed Pashmina shawls. Ladakhi Pashmina is usually grey or brown and the animal husbandry department is attempting to create more of the white wool which is far superior and more expensive.

The road between Upshi and Leh lies through an uncultivated plain, now disturbed by the civil works for the Stakna project and road building activity. Snow-

The image shows a sign in Devanagari script: हिमांक परियोजना / खरटुंगला / दुनिया की सबसे / ऊँची सड़क / ऊँचाई 18380 फीट / 16TF / 54RCC / जते

FACING PAGE: LAHUL IS A POPULAR TREKKING DESTINATION BECAUSE OF THE NUMEROUS SNOW-COVERED PEAKS THAT APPEAR AND DISAPPEAR IN THE CLOUDS.

AT A HEIGHT OF 18,380 FEET, KHARDUNG-LA PASS IS THE HIGHEST MOTORABLE ROAD IN THE WORLD.

covered mountains enclose the plain as the road crosses and recesses between the banks of the river. The poplar parks and fields closer to Leh are representative of the benefits of irrigation for the villages that lie near the river bed. Here it is possible to taste gur gur tea, a salted mix of Tibetan tea and butter churned in beautifully carved containers and served in equally beautiful samovars. Pinkish in colour, it tastes like weak broth and is extremely refreshing in the dry climate and replenishes energy at high altitudes. The Chemrye monastery is a short distance away and well worth a stop. Stakna, Mahto and Thikse are other monasteries that beckon the visitor off the road.

The extensive Chu-shot valley is a pastoral dream of houses and farms. The flat roofs covered with firewood and fodder, the walls washed white and studded with pretty balconies, are in sharp relief to the rugged landscape. The industry of women is evident in the fields, whilst the men lend a hand in threshing if they are not away on a trade mission. A typical meal of salted tea, wheat cakes, Tibetan biscuits, Ladakhi apricots and Kashmiri grapes gives one a flavour of the past when Leh was an entrepot on the old silk route. It was common to see Chabba traders from Lhasa arrive on yaks laden with tea, caravans from Yarkhand carrying wool, felts and silk as well as sturdy horses with deep chests and strong

forelegs which were prized in Punjab, a frontier region of India. Today, the exotic has given way to a Tibetan market where smuggled goods from Nepal and China sell alongside the produce of Punjab and Kashmir.

The road to Leh is a sandy ascent completely devoid of vegetation. *Mane* walls lead to a large *chorten,* embellished with copper, gold and silk, that stands guard at the entrance to the town. The south-east and north-west axis of the Indus valley where Leh stands continues to Dras and the frontiers of the Kashmir valley. To the north-east, at an elevation of 11,000 ft, lies the Nubra valley, 2,000 ft higher than Leh. The Rudok valley is another major watershed for the Shyok river, the winter road for Balti traders before the occupation of Kashmir by Pakistan.

The Zanskar joins the Indus river from the south at Nyemo. This is the great drain through which the snows from the lofty Tibetan plateau come down to fertilise the plains of Punjab. The speed and force of the rivers is due to the strong current and not due to their depth. This region is now being exploited for white-water rafting, a popular tourist activity in the Himalaya.

Given the broken surface of Ladakh, cultivation is possible at levels that border the streams and on the lower slopes of the hills. The soil consists almost entirely of pulverised rocks; the mountains being primitive, the decomposition of granite clothes the fields with a coating of clay, sand, gravel and pebbles. The peasants therefore have to work extremely hard. But the interesting feature of this soil is that it yields abundant crops year after year, without any crop rotation or the need to leave land fallow.

A VENDOR WEIGHING DRIED TOMATOES AT THE LEH MARKET, LADAKH.

FACING PAGE: A NUN COOKING POTATOES IN KARSHA MONASTERY IN ZANSKAR, LADAKH.

69

When fields are cleared for cultivation, the large rocks are left undisturbed, whilst the shards are collected to enclose the fields within the characteristic stone walls, to create terraces which are then linked to streams or springs on higher ground for irrigation. Terraces on higher slopes are formed by catching debris from melting snows and leaving it for nature to act upon for future generations. This practice has helped to expand the inhabited area in these otherwise sterile valleys.

The general appearance of Ladakh is one of extreme barrenness: inhabited by poplars and furze or a few tufts of wormwood, dog rose and other desert plants. The rocks seem to enhance the barrenness of the soil. The climate is equally uncompromising. Frost, snow and sleet commence in September and continue till May, with extremely low temperatures between December and February. Ice coats the surface of the streams even in May and June. Between July and August, the summer sun is intensely hot and temperatures can reach 40 degrees centigrade. This heat rapidly matures the crops, and barley, the staple in these high altitudes, ripens for harvesting within two months of sowing.

Wheat, known as *to*, is a common crop and the Tibetan variety known as *to karma* is very hardy and productive. It gives very little straw, unlike the *hasora* variety grown to the west. The straw is often plaited by the women to make caps, decorative items for the hair, which are still used by the Drok-pas or the Dards who live

SNOW-COVERED *CHORTENS* IN LEH, LADAKH. *CHORTENS* ARE
TIBETAN BUDDHIST RELIQUARIES, MEMORIALS TO THE
TEACHINGS OF THE BUDDHA.

A HERD OF GOATS SKID DOWNHILL AS THEY RETURN FROM THE HIGH PASTURES.

north of the Suru valley. The six-variety naked barley, known as *sherokh*, is extremely suitable for the cold climate. It is alternated with buck wheat for a second crop in the intense summer. Since Ladakhi cuisine is flour-based, as is the popular beverage *chang*, a kind of barley beer brewed in every house, grain is the major agricultural produce. For harvesting, the plant is either pulled up from the roots just before maturity or cut with a sickle so designed that the hand of the peasant does not get scraped by the gravelly soil. Fodder is supplemented with lucerne, called *olh* or *champu*, which is stored on the roof of every Ladakhi house.

Onions, carrots, turnips and cabbage form the vegetable store and are dried for winter use. Rhubarb is another valuable vegetable found mainly in the Chang Thang plateau. Earlier, it was imported from China for its medicinal value and for dyeing. Apricots and apples are the only fruit grown but there are at least ten varieties of apricots which long ago were dried and carried by the traders along with *sattu* (barley flour) on the long marches out of Leh. Apricot seeds also yield sweet almonds. Saspul, on the banks of the Indus, is a beautiful village with its apricot orchards. The sarsinh tree yields a fragrant flower which is a prized form of perfume for the local people. Its fruit which resembles an olive or a *ber* (an Indian berry) is considered a delicacy since it is not found very commonly. When dried, the powder is used to make sherbet. Its fermented form gives a brandy which is popular in Yarkhand. Balti pears were popular as were the melons of Yarkhand. Now fruit is brought in from the south of the Himalaya, since the borders are closed.

All Ladakhi villages had willow or poplar plantations since fuel was required for the long winter. This practice has not been kept up since coal is replacing wood, despite the fact that it comes to Ladakh at a much higher price. The yaks of Ladakh are not as impressive as those from Chang Thang, but they are extremely docile. Similarly, the Purik sheep, kept for shawl wool and homespun cloth, are much smaller than the Chang Thang breeds. This domesticated sheep pastures in the mountains in the summer but in the winter is like a pet dog looking for table scraps.

The Chang Thang goat whose fleece provides the famous Pashmina for the Kashmiri shawl is now a protected species. The hair of the Pashmina goat is used for ropes, sacks and blankets for home consumption. Wild animals include the ibex whose horns adorn homes and mountain shrines (*nazars*) as charms to ward off the evil eye. There is the blue sheep and the highly elusive *kiang*. Hare and marmots, lynx, foxes and snow leopards can be glimpsed in the mountains. Road works have disturbed the traditional burrows and in summer it is possible to see these animals near the roads. A high altitude national park has been established to protect the snow leopard, an extremely shy animal. The Stok Nallah is a good spot to view some of the wildlife near Leh. It is a comfortable trek and a popular camping area. Ravens, chakhors, sparrows, linnets and robins are visible during harvest time, whilst the crested skylark and the snowlark are found in the higher mountains. Visitors have often mistaken their songs for human voices. Water birds and fish abound in the lakes but the Buddhists do not touch them.

The mineral wealth of Nubra and Chang Thang is well known, particularly the rich deposits of sulphur and

TRADERS RETURN TO SPITI, THEIR YAKS LOADED WITH SUPPLIES.

gold. But none of this is being excavated as lamas have declared that it will lead to a bad harvest.

Leh stands on the northern boundary of the Indus plain. Once a walled town, much of its fortifications have now fallen apart. Only a few conical and square towers stand guard over the summits. The city is approached by a double line of sacred walls or *manes*. Earlier outlying houses had no walls and the doors were never locked or bolted. Now mud brick walls protect them. In the old town, which forms a heritage zone, the streets form a labyrinth with houses running into each other, so that from the outside it is difficult to estimate the size of the mansion.

Generally two to three storeys high, with walls of unburnt bricks, houses are sometimes white washed on the outside but retain their mud plaster on the inside. Light wooden balconies on the upper floors add to their charm. The roofs are flat, formed by small poplar trunks, with a covering of willow shoots and a coating of straw. Although State-sponsored PWD architecture and modern city designs can be seen in plenty, Leh still retains its original flavour. In the traditional homes, rooms are large with low ceilings. In the houses of the rich, the ceilings are made of wood, often in a lozenge pattern, and varnished. Pillars holding up painted and varnished columns and capitals are replaced by capitals of straw and wheat in peasant homes.

The most remarkable building in Leh is the seven-storeyed Palace below which the old town straggles down to the riverine plain. Most of its wooden capitals and columns had been vandalised for fuel and weathering has washed away the murals. But the Palace has been acquired from the late king's widow by the archaeological survey department and is being reconstructed. The Palace is the prototype of the Po-tala palace in Tibet. Its 250 ft is broken by slit windows which are a source of light and protect against the cold. The courtyard near the *gompa* is used for theatre performances by the North Zone Cultural Centre, since the rocks form a natural amphitheatre.

The monasteries are built in the same way as the mansions, since they form a part of the civil and military administration. Each monastery controls a number of villages and combines the functions of a landlord with those of money-lending, trade and barter. Through the conversion of tribal customs and practices into Buddhist rituals, and in the transformation of the totemic Bon culture, the monasteries became more formal and institutionalised, and the infrastructure was consolidated

HEAVEN AND EARTH SEEM TO MEET AT THE TSO MORARI LAKE IN NORTHERN LADAKH, HOME TO THE BAR-HEADED GEESE.

KYE MONASTERY, THE LARGEST IN SPITI, IS A TYPICAL EXAMPLE OF THE FORTRESS MONASTERY. ITS BASEMENT CONTAINS A RARE COLLECTION OF ARMS, A REMINDER OF ITS TURBULENT PAST.

with the increasing wealth accumulated through their growing power. They also became the focus of cultural activities providing skills in literacy, medicine, fine art, philosophy and astrology. The monasteries' maintenance, repair and ornamentation have improved since tourists began to visit Ladakh in large numbers. They are raising money by holding festivals in the summer when tourists buy tickets to see the traditional Cham dances.

On the eastern frontier of Leh is the sandy plateau of Chang Thang, spotted with salt-lakes and pastures. The Rudokh fort and Pangong lake dominate the sparsely populated Chusul valley. Most of its people are shepherds who subsist on the sale of wool to Leh merchants. The road north of Rudokh leads to Khotan and to the south lie Sumgiel and Tholing, bordering Spiti and Kinnaur. Garo is the main connecting link on the Indus towards Ladakh. Market stops and shepherd stations make one feel that time has stood still on the road to Gartokh. This region still has strong links with Tibet although its lamas are no longer sent by the Dalai Lama, who is now in India. Formerly there was extensive trade between Khotan and Ladakh, but political changes have all but destroyed it.

HUNDREDS OF PRAYER FLAGS STRUNG UP
OVER A BOULDER AT RHOTANG-PASS.

The route to Nubra valley now goes over the high pass, the Khardong-la, but previously, it passed through the royal village of Sabu, a more pleasant and fertile region than Leh. The ascent on both routes is extremely steep and fatiguing and the difficulty in breathing is acute. Not just men but even horses and yaks are known to pass out at this great height. The road is a tumbled mess of sand, gravel and rock, the sun is powerful and the vista an impregnable wall of mountains.

The local people wear a plait of yak's hair across the forehead to protect their eyes from the sun. Digar, Lokjum and Tagar, villages that emerge magically from the sand and rubble of the mountain, have red stone pillars outside every house to ward off evil. Here, sand ridges are formed and reformed by the high velocity winds that howl through the plain. Some distance away, at Tarsha, we come upon the hot springs which flow out of the mountain ridge. The openings are small and the water flows gently, in a clear stream. Simple baths made of stone walls collect the water and crusts of soda called *phul* are used as soap.

TRADERS WINDING UP THEIR CAMP AS THEY RETURN HOME.

South-east of the Rupshu plain lies the old road to Spiti. Here, the soil is made of loose clay or micaceous sand scattered over with stones. Thin patches of furze provide pasturage for the flocks of sheep and goats. The *mane* walls are the only imprint of human passage. Whirlwinds are common on this plain: sand rises in a column to a great height whilst all around it the air is calm and still. The road passes the Tso Morari lake, deeper than Pangong but less clear. There is no sign of life here and although water courses fill the lake, its level seems to be maintained purely by evaporation.

The nomads of Spiti and Rupshu meet at Parang-la for their barter trade. The women are adorned in the traditional Chang Thang fashion with a *perak,* a head-dress shaped like a cobra-hood and studded with turquoise. The men wear caps trimmed with fur. The Parang-la is one of the narrowest and the most difficult to cross, but it leads into a fertile valley. The Losar and Pin rivers create a broad valley which terminates at the steep slopes of the Dhankar fortress. The Key Gompa lies a day's journey from here. These heights have been the battleground for the rulers of Leh, Chamba and Kullu, since each one wanted control of the shawl wool trade.

Kaza, Tabo and Pin form a triangle which is the core area of interest and habitation in Spiti. A few landholding families control the political and economic power of the region. In recent times, development in the form of tourism and anti-desertification programmes have brought in changes that have undermined the barter economy. Family, culture and traditional forms of

IN TIBET ART AND RELIGION GO HAND IN HAND. WOOD IS WIDELY USED, INTRICATELY CARVED AND BRIGHTLY PAINTED FOR ENTRANCES TO HOMES AND MONASTERIES.

socialisation have given way under the pressure of modernisation. However, the Spiti tourism authority has taken up the challenge of the new situation and hopes to realise the benefits of modernisation through monitoring and controlling the pace of change.

The boundary between Kinnaur and Spiti is formed by the Spiti and Pare rivers near the Indo-Tibetan border. Upper Kinnaur is in the arid Trans Himalayan region. Three roughly parallel ranges run in Kinnaur: the Zanskar, the Great Himalayan Range and the Dhauladhar. The legendary Pandavas of the *Mahabharata* (world's longest epic in which the five Pandava brothers fought their cousins, the Kauravas, to regain the kingdom of Hastinapur) are said to have built many mud forts in the Baspa valley during the period of their exile. Hereditary oracles recount the oral history of Kinnaur, known as *chironings*, where myth and reality are hard to distinguish. For instance, the legendary king Banasur is said to have brought the Sutlej river to the plains from Lake Mansarovar; the topography seems to suggest the forcing of the river through the wall of a rock.

Kinnaur lies in the valley of the Trans Himalayan river Sutlej and its tributary, the Baspa. It is renowned for the Kinner Kailash Yatra, a four-day trek that is undertaken by both the Buddhists and the Hindus. The northeast-southwest orientation of the Baspa valley follows the Himalayan drift. The north-east is arid, whilst the south-west is a veritable garden. Entering the valley at Chit-kul, we can observe millions of butterflies and alpine flowers. Here, the Ge-lug-pa sect has a monastery; the mane walls and *chortens* leading to the rotating prayer wheels which travellers visit before climbing to the higher ranges. Legend has it that the Baspa was a pre-historic lake, and a hydro-electric project is set to make the legend come true. The Hangrang valley, which borders Tibet, is extremely rugged and barren in contrast.

Nomadic shepherds inhabit the small villages here. Kinnaur was renowned for the town of Nichar, accessed by the Indo-Tibet border road, which still provides rest and refreshment to the travellers. Kalpa offers incredible views of the snow and being less dry than the core desert, is surrounded by dry pine and *chilgoza* (fruit pine) forests. Pooh is a small town located in the core desert zone and receives 40 cm of rain and snow in a year. Barren mountains and large scree slopes give Pooh its characteristic lunar landscape. Moorang is another small settlement in the cold desert zone, although its lower elevation makes it slightly warmer. Traditionally, in each settlement, lamas were responsible for the care of travellers whilst the nuns carried on the tasks of chanting prayers, printing sacred texts and performing the daily tasks. Lamas continue to direct the welfare of the people regardless of their religion, whether it is the starting of the agricultural season, fixing the date of a marriage, the leave-taking of the nomadic shepherds, the birth of a child or the death of an old resident.

The life of the nomads, so frequently encountered here, is hard. They are simple, superstitious people who live in tents made from rough blankets. The tents are simply furnished with goat and sheep skin which are roughly stitched together to make winter coats. A few iron cooking pots complete their possessions. Goat-skin

MARSH MARIGOLDS (*COLTA PALUSTRIS*) HERALDING THE BEGINNING OF SPRING IN LADAKH.

bags hold cream and butter for the salted tea that is an essential requirement at the heights which they go in search of pasture. Their clothes are made of homespun woolen cloth, woven in long narrow strips, one end of the loom tied to the waist of the weaver and the other attached to a stone.

Since cultivable land was scarce, polyandry was practised in most of the region so that the holdings were not fragmented. Myth links this practice to the Pandava brothers who married Draupadi, but the basis of polyandry is clearly economic. However, monogamy has become the norm amongst the urban communities today and is also influencing rural patterns of marriage and family tradition.

The mountains are all of blue slate, steep and naked to the top. Their barrenness and decay is frightful. The road follows the bed of the river and is passable only in the winter. In summer, the steep gradient makes the passes accessible only to the most experienced. The red hat sect of Buddhists predominates here; the people are extremely superstitious and each house has a charm in the form of a yak's tail or a flag painted with *mantras*. Stalks of barley hang upside down on every door. The *mane* walls which indicate that a passage is possible, are always crossed from the right side so that the mantra - *Om Mane Padma Om* - is not read backwards. Prayer wheels when not turned by pilgrims are moved by the wind.

Snow melt is scanty and therefore vegetation is of the dwarf variety. Clouds flit over the peaks as misty vapour and roll down the slopes, dispersing into invisibility. Brilliant minerals arrest the eye of the traveller, as does the steep incline of the granite cliffs. Lamas have maintained the rope bridges and some temples have pagoda-like forms that indicate the Chinese influence in Kinnaur before it was handed over to Bushar. These are quite different from the flat roofs in the rest of the region.

Visitors are fascinated by the impregnable massif of the Himalaya because travellers have narrated, documented and added to the metaphysical attraction of the high mountains, their ridges interrupted by passes. Buddhism has endured along with the merchant and the conqueror, and created a spiritual aura that personifies the peaks and creates an interaction between the valleys. The dependence on barter economy, has created a sharing of information, ideas, technology and festivals that strengthen the ties between people who have braved the cold deserts, to live in the valleys protected by gods.

THE MANALLA ROAD LEADING THROUGH SPITI VALLEY TO THE KI GOMPA IS PASSABLE FOR NO MORE THAN TWO OR THREE MONTHS A YEAR.

FOLLOWING PAGE 84: THE ELABORATELY ORNAMENTED AND IMPOSING IMAGE OF *CHHAMBA* (MAITREYA BUDDHA) AT THE THIKSE MONASTERY.

BUDDHISM:
THE CREATOR
AND PRESERVER OF
THE HIMALAYAN
KINGDOMS

In the political and cultural cross-currents that buffeted the Western Himalaya, it was not just geography or climate that determined the regional identity of the people. The deepest impact was inspired by the spread of Buddhism. The lama and the *raja* made an alliance that survived the ups and downs of history. By imposing the law of Dharma, the peasant and the trader were made to support the monastic order. The wealth husbanded by the monastery brought about social stability as well as the development of art and architecture through out the region.

Buddhism has had a tenacious hold on the people of these hill regions because the outsider is a temporary visitor. It is religion which has sustained the local people through the violent upheavals and the bitter cold, which determined the daily routine, the seasonal activity and the rites of passage. Even today, oil lamps are lit in the family temple, scriptures recited and *Om Mane Padma Om* chanted with devotion and fervour.

Buddhism developed in the Western Himalaya in two phases. The first phase was its introduction and propagation by Indian monks and visits by Tibetan scholars to the *mahaviharas* (universities) of Nalanda, Odantapura and Vikramsila. The establishment of the Sam-ya monastery in Tibet in 722 AD is credited to the Indian monk Padmasambhava, regarded as the second Buddha due to his role in the propogation of Buddhism. The second phase was what the Tibetans call the Second Advancement. This process was centred on the central

AN ORACLE INFLICTING WOUNDS ON HIMSELF DURING THE ANNUAL ORACLE FESTIVAL AT MATHO MONASTERY.

Tibetan kingdom of Gu-je, which included the kingdoms of Lahul and Spiti and parts of Kinnaur.

However, it should not to be assumed that Buddhism spread through peaceful missionary activity. Between the fifth and the tenth centuries, it established itself and emerged as a pan-Asian religion through guile, conversion and the elevation of clan chiefs to kingship. Songsen Gampo, the first Buddhist king of Tibet, used his marriage alliance with the princesses of Nepal and China to beat his rival clansmen to the throne. It were these princesses who brought the political and religious features of Buddhism to Tibet. In time, Tibet became a Buddhist theocracy, with the Dalai Lama as the temporal and spiritual leader.

Ladakh is often called Little Tibet because the form of Buddhism here is closely linked to that of Tibet; both Leh and Tabo recently celebrated thousand years' of ties with Tibet. Though the Dalai Lama now resides in India, the Tibetan teachers have adhered faithfully to the teachings of the Buddha enshrined in the sacred Indian texts that pilgrims and monks carried with them far and wide.

The commentaries on the tenets of basic Buddhism as they were handed down from generation to generation, have been termed Nikaya, Mahayana and Tantric forms of Buddhism. Mahayana or the Great Wheel, which believes in the possibility of salvation for all, spread to Tibet in the seventh and eighth centuries. When Tibetan influence increased in the eleventh century, this form of Buddhism adapted to the Tibetan schools.

The appeal of Mahayana was that it allowed salvation through *bhakti* (devotion) and the vow of religious discipline, while living the life of a lay man. From this concept emerged the *Bodhisattva*, the being who held back his salvation so that he may help others seek the path of enlightenment. Once the Buddha became the Saviour, a pantheon of deities developed. This brought about a change in the representation of the Buddha as well as the social role of the monastery.

The hierarchy of deities, each approached by the recitation of a specific *mantra* (ritual speech), led to a personified form of representation as against the symbolic form practised earlier. Stories from the life and times of the Buddha also found expression in literature and the oral tradition of knowledge was replaced by written texts. The *Tanjur* (1,108 texts) and the *Kanjur* (3,461 texts) came into being which can be found in the libraries of the monasteries at Phiyang and Shashur. Knowledge of these scriptures was most important for the monks. The Chinese traveller Hsuan-tsang noted: 'He who can explain one class of these books is exempted from the control of Karmadana. If he can explain two classes, he receives the assignment of an upper seat. He who can explain four classes has lay followers. He who can explain five classes is allowed an escort... If one of the assembly distinguishes himself by refined language, subtle investigation, deep penetration and severe logic, then he is mounted on an elephant and conducted in procession through the gates of the monastery. If one of

FACING PAGE: A BONPO MONK IN DARK RETREAT IN LUBROK, MUSTANG.

THE MONASTERIES OF
MUSTANG, NEPAL
CONTAIN SOME OF THE
LAST REMAINING RELICS
OF AN ALMOST VANISHED
WORLD OF ANCIENT
BUDDHIST CULTURE.

THE IMAGE OF PADMASAMBHAVA AT THE HEMIS *GOMPA* IN LADAKH.

the members breaks down in argument, or uses poor and inelegant language, his face is disfigured with red and white and his body covered with dust and he is carried off to some deserted spot and thrown into a ditch.'

One is reminded of these words as young novices recite the texts under the vigilant eye of the abbot who walks between the rows of chanting lamas brandishing a horsewhip. The rigours of teaching brought to Tibet by the Indian *acharyas* (teachers) Padmasambhava and Atisa, and later introduced to Ladakh by Rin-chen Zang-po, continue in the monasteries of the region even today.

The core of Buddhism was the Sangha, the order, which centred itself on the *vihara* or monastery and the *mahavihara* or the university. This was the concept of the Triple Gem that the Buddha required of every disciple. The Sangha became an extremely sophisticated organisation by the time the large monasteries of Tibet like Tashilumpo Ganden and Dera were established. Modelled on the *bhiku* or almsman, the Sangha evolved from the haphazard, independent existence of the *bhiku* into an organised collective with common aims and discipline.

The *vinaya* or monastic way of life evolved from the institution of *vassavasa* or rain retreat which gave the wandering *bhikus* an opportunity to meet other monks and experience a communal life. From a temporary resting place away from the laity, there emerged the *avasa* or rural retreat and the *arama*, the urban retreat. The former required the monks to be self-sufficient whereas in the latter they could accept patronage of the local community. The *arama* was founded on land donated by the patron and had a boundary wall which enclosed the dwellings. This evolved into the *sangharama* where the patron could be invited to take part in discussions relating to the teachings of the Buddha. The boundary walls soon enclosed assembly halls, temples and spaces for *parikrama* rituals. As links with the merchant-patron grew, monastic art and architecture reached great sophistication because of the resources that were made available to give permanence to these institutions. Construction which had followed the Indian prototype developed from wood and brick to rock and stone. Even today, the foundation is of stone with wooden beams, stone columns and mud walls.

As the *sangharama* transformed into the *lena*, there was increasing formalisation of the monastic order. Apart from the teaching and care of monks and novices, contact with the community also had to be established.

As Buddhism matured, the teachings of the Buddha came to be interpreted variously which led to sectarianism. Buddhist texts were written in Sanskrit and required translation. King Songsen Gampo developed the practice of inviting monks and scholars from India to translate these works and also teach them to his people. Padmasambhava, who is represented in many icons in the monasteries of the region, came to Tibet in the eighth century. His followers are known as the Nying-ma pa or the ancient ones. Milrepa, a teacher of the eleventh century founded the Ka-gyud pa sect, known as the profound ones. In the fourteenth century, there emerged in Tibet a reformist sect known as the Ge-lugs pa or the virtuous ones. The first monk of this sect, Tsong-kha pa is renowned for his teachings and the sect is famous as the

CHOM OR MASKED DANCERS AT THE MATHO MONASTERY FESTIVAL IN LADAKH.

yellow hat sect. The Dalai Lama belongs to this sect. In Ladakh, a sub-sect of the Ka-gyud pa called the Duk-pa, along with the Ge-lugs pa, gained prominence. Hemis, which is the premier monastery of the Duk-pa order, controls several smaller monasteries in the Indus valley and Zanskar. Spituk, Thikse and Likir, the most historic monasteries of the region, belong to the Ge-lugs pa sect. Alchi, perhaps the most extraordinary Buddhist *gompa* in the Indus valley and justly renowned for its murals, belonged to an obsolete order, Ka-dam pa, which was prominent in the eleventh century.

Ladakhis are, however, not sectarian. They revere the teachings of the Buddha regardless of the sect, and villages have adherents of all prominent beliefs. The *Lha-khang* or sacred shrine in the family home is a constant reminder to the people to tread the noble path. Lamas come once a month to offer special prayers for the family. No event is complete without the presence of the lamas and all major decisions are taken with their advice and consent. The spiritual presence of the monastery and monks in the heart of the community is a representation of the spirit of Buddhism that dominates our consciousness when we are in the region.

The multifunctional Odantapura was the model for the earliest Tibetan monastery Sam-ya, which then became the prototype for all the monasteries constructed in the Himalaya. The central temple rooms were only a small part of the complex. Teaching blocks and residential apartments were enclosed by a wall that had

FACING PAGE: THE EXQUISITELY CARVED IMAGE OF MAITREYA, THE BUDDHA YET TO COME.

four gates at the cardinal points. The *chaityas* (large arched openings) on the walls were covered with inscriptions. To the left of the main chapel door was a large painting of the wheel of life. The complex was built on the *mandala* plan (geometric diagram representing the universe) oriented towards the cardinal points. The central temple was three-tiered, conforming to the style prevalent in India, China and Tibet. In an adjacent enclosure, the demons had a space to devour humans who were not protected. Despite the destruction unleashed by King Lang Dar Ma in the ninth century to revive the Bon religion, it is claimed that he could not destroy the sacred images which had magical powers.

According to Tibetan texts, a goat-herd named Kar gyal, inspired by a Naga, began preaching a strange religion (a form of Bonism) which was opposed to Buddhism. Rin-chen Zang-po overcame him and also suppressed some of the *tantriks* (religious men with occult powers) who under the garb of religion were committing obscenities. By purifying the sacred religion Rin-chen gained the confidence of the people and Buddhism survived.

Most of the temples in the Second Advancement period were constructed in Kinnaur, Spiti and western Gu-je. In the year 990 AD, King Ye-she-od became a monk and built the monastery at Tholing. Rin-chen Zang-po was the first abbot of this monastery which was modelled on Sam-ya. In 996 AD, the duo founded Tabo. In 1010 AD, the two brothers of the king who were also monks, invited the Indian *acharya* Atisa to Tibet. They restored Tabo and set up the Mangang *gompa*. These are the only evidences of Indo-Tibetan architectural heritage in the Himalaya. This period also saw the penetration of artistic and cultural influences from the Buddhist kingdom of Kashmir, from which we can trace the West Asian influences that are evident in the Western Himalaya and western Tibet.

The later complexes built in the fourteenth and fifteenth centuries by the Ge-lugs pa are however different. The multifunctional monastery complexes had by now become centres of rival political power,

a manifestation of sectarianism. The fortified monasteries are a product of this period. These were perched on hill tops, hidden in gullies or carved into rocks or sandy plains so that access became difficult. A comparison of Alchi or Tabo monastery with Hemis or Phiyang makes this difference clear. Lamayuru monastery towers above Senge-sgang, where the boundary wall acts as a symbolic barrier circumscribed by a band of flames, lotus petals and a belt of diamonds.

The early temples were dedicated to the Vairocana (white) Buddha, always found in the centre with the five *tathagathas* (future Buddhas): Akshobhya (blue) to the east, Ratnasambhava (yellow) to the south, Amitabha (red) to the west and Amoghasiddha (green) to

A MONK CLOSING THE DOORS IN LADAKH'S ALCHI MONASTERY, FOUNDED IN THE ELEVENTH CENTURY BY THE 'GREAT TRANSLATOR', RIN-CHEN ZANG-PO. THIS EXQUISTELY PAINTED AND CARVED MONASTERY IS ONE OF THE MOST IMPORTANT CENTRES OF BUDDHIST ART IN LADAKH.

the north. The cult of Vairocana was rare in Tibet. The Vairocana *mandala* has 37 divinities including the *tathagathas*, the four *shaktis* (female divinities) of whom the Tara of the north-east is the most famous, eight subsidiary goddesses (*vajras*), sixteen *bodhisattvas* belonging to the Vajra, Ratna, Padma and Visvavajra families and the four guardians covering the cardinal points. Many of the decorative *mandala* motifs are influenced by Byzantine-Syrian art.

MONKS BLOWING TRUMPET HORNS AT THE ANNUAL FESTIVAL IN SPITUK MONASTERY.

The Lha-lun temple near Dhankar in Spiti is well preserved and one can see the features of the early period reflected in its east-west orientation and layout. As the hegemony of the Ge-lugs pa strengthened, the socio-cultural links with India were weakened and the lamas reoriented themselves to Lhasa. Later monasteries were closely linked to the programme of territorial expansion. The defeat of the tribal chiefs was achieved by superior arms and tactics learnt through Buddhist cultural links forged with both India and China. Thus, the fort and the monastery became the military and administrative units and began to be combined.

The civil function of the *gompa* was discharged through the land ownership system, where a number of villages were under the administrative control of the monasteries. Monasteries owned land in the villages which they leased out on a crop-sharing basis. This surplus was converted into silver, gold and art treasures.

The monastery extended its control to bartering, money-lending, trade and mortgaging. Tribal customs and festivals were transformed into *gompa* festivals. Tribal beliefs and knowledge were also appropriated and given a basis in Buddhist theology, not ridiculed as mere superstition. The system of primogeniture helped to keep the monastery system alive as every family in the village provided a novice. Thikse, Phiyang, Likir, Basgo, Lamayuru, Karsha, Kye, Tanjur and Dhankar all follow this pattern.

In the newer monasteries, the *Du-khang* or assembly room is the largest and central to the complex, since the Ge-lugs pa follow the Mahayana tradition. However, the rigid adherence to canonical laws of the *mandala* system are now replaced by a haphazard arrangement of deities on the walls and the altar. The features of the icons are much more Mongoloid and decorative. Aspects like clouds, flowers and landscapes recall the Chinese influence. The interesting feature of these monasteries is that each household maintains a cell in the residential quarters, for those who join as novices, and the householder provides for their sustenance. The social and economic links are thus strengthened.

Buddhist architecture has now moved away from the four-way orientation of Sam-ya to the one-way orientation of the early monasteries facing the altar. There is a physical division here between the temple complex and the secular structures. The newer *gompas* are built around a court with the temple placed in the centre. In Ladakh and Spiti, one sees a fourth type of complex with individual buildings spread across the top and sides of a

FOUNDED IN 996 AD, TABO GOMPA IN SPITI IS THE OLDEST LIVING MONASTERY. ONLY A PART OF THE OLD STRUCTURE REMAINS TODAY, SINCE MUCH OF IT WAS DESTROYED IN A MASSIVE EARTHQUAKE THAT STRUCK THE REGION IN 1975.

FACING PAGE: TREKKERS NEGOTIATING THE STEEP DESCENT TO THE FROZEN ZANSKAR RIVER IN LADAKH.

hillock with no symmetrical axis or arrangement. This style was created more for defence than for symbolic representation. Spituk is a good example of this type of structure. Rid-zong, Kye and Dhankar monasteries were reconstructed according to the new concept once they were taken over. Shankar in Leh and others in Nubra and Chang Thang also follow this pattern.

The new style is recognisable by the temple at the highest elevation, identified by the flags and umbrella on its roof. The walls are white and sloping, with slit windows framed in black and timber balconies at upper levels. The courtyard through which the temple is entered is the space for *cham* dances and other festivals. The *parikrama* is performed in a covered passage which surrounds the temple. This tradition is linked to *stupa* architecture. The corridor or space around the temple often has a row of prayer wheels at elbow level and it is customary to turn the wheel once, thrice or one hundred and eight times. There is a portico that symbolically separates the temple from the world beyond. The gateway is protected by the four guardians: Dhritarashtra (white, with a stringed instrument) on the east, Virudhaka (blue or green, with a sword) on the south, Virupaksha (red with a *chorten*, a serpent or a jewel) on west and Kuvera (yellow and carrying a banner in the right hand and a mongoose in the left) on the north.

In addition, the eight glorious signs are painted in the porch. These are two gold fish, an umbrella, a conch shell, a symbolic diagram, banner, vase, lotus and the wheel of law. The *Du-khang* has images on the short wall opposite the entrance so that two rows of monks can be accommodated before the head lama who always sits to the right of the image, on a raised platform. Some monasteries have large images which recall the tradition of the cave temples at Bamian. The *Gon-khang* houses the malevolent deities and has protective devices on the door. The *Gon-khangs* at Phiyang and Thikse have murals of monks of the old Ka-gyu pa sect and the terrifying Lah-mo forms of gods. The monks' cells, large kitchens and *chortens* make up the rest of the complex. These have eight forms: unity in diversity, magical power, descent from heaven, emanation of happiness, victory, nirvana, enlightenment and a bunch/mound of lotuses. Of these, the divine manifestation and enlightenment forms are the most common. The *Lha-khang* houses the *Kanjur* and the *Tanjur*.

Lahul is primarily controlled by the Druk-pa sect. The most interesting temple here is that of Guru Ghantal situated above the confluence of the Chandra and Bhaga rivers at Tandi. The monks officiating here come from Stakna in Ladakh. Its pyramidal roof is distinctly decorated with a *mandala* pattern and is older than the slate roof from Kangra. There is a sealed room which today contains only rocks. The dormer door is decorated with Celtic, Byzantine and Hellenistic designs, perhaps created by the craftsmen brought from different parts of the world by king Lalita Muktapada.

Monastery records, all of which have not been plundered or lost, have to be documented and translated if we are to have more than a cursory knowledge of the history of the region and its monastic institutions. They are bound to have a detailed history of the area which would enrich our knowledge of the region's heritage. At present, our source of information is the oral history of the local religious and social elite. International scholars have generally ignored the wealth of art and culture of the Western Himalaya because of their fascination with Central Asia.

THE KARMA AND DHARMA OF DAILY LIFE

The Kesar Saga, a richly detailed narrative of the life and times of the Ladakhi hero Gyapo Kesar, has been passed down in the tradition of story telling from one generation to the next. While keeping to the spirit of the epic, many new tales have been added which tell us a great deal about the changes that have come about in the cultural history of the high desert areas.

Ladakh does not need to transform to modern systems which are very difficult to maintain at such heights. However, no culture can remain isolated. As changes occur, the people of these valleys continue to absorb all new inputs into their social and spiritual framework. Where change has been of doubtful value, as in Spiti and Mustang, it has been due to unrestricted tourism. Mountain people have survived because they were capable of healthy adaptability, since they could control outsiders by limiting their entry. Tourism, however, is now penetrating into the private sphere and threatening the very *dharma* of their lives.

Today, the Ladakhis have shifted to the extended family system. They no longer follow the tradition of the *Khang bu*, where the elder couple move to a hermitage to allow the younger ones to stand on their feet. This change is a result of the increasing wealth of the land-owning families and of Muslim culture, which does not follow the noble path of the rites of passage. Changes have also occurred in the self-sufficiency of the household which used to produce all its needs. Today, the domestic market

THE LADAKHIS HAVE AN INCREDIBLE CAPACITY TO ASSIMILATE AND CHANGE WITH THE TIMES. PRIMITIVE MUD STOVES HAVE BEEN REPLACED BY COPPER OR IRON ONES.

sells products made all over India and there is much more dependence on it than in earlier times.

What remains unchanged is the rhythm of the seasons. Spring and summer are the months of agricultural activity. Autumn is the time for collecting fuel for the long winter. Here again, tourism has intervened. The monastery festivals which gave people the opportunity to replenish their winter stocks have been shifted to the summer, so that monasteries can earn an income since they no longer control trade. Now families spend their time making ropes, weaving carpets and baskets and of course, running the civil administration which has been taken over by the secular state. The *Kahlon* has been superseded by the district collector.

LADAKHI ROADWORKERS REFRESH
THEMSELVES WITH A CUP OF HOT
SALTED BUTTER TEA.

Mountains dominate the life cycle. The village that has a mountain in the rear is fortunate, because the snow melt provides the water of life to it. The June heat brings a steady stream of water in a happy, gurgling race down the slopes to the well ploughed fields below. Earlier, each village was divided into sections with its appointed *go-pa* who ensured proper sharing of water. Now the district administration has replaced the traditional system and the *scurrim-ba* or water festival which celebrates the first snow melt, is often the scene of conflict between farmers and hoteliers who are opening for the tourist season.

Where towns are distant, bartering willow for grain still continues. Barley from the uplands is also bartered for wheat from the valley, used for *tagi* (a form of bread) which is a necessary food at high altitudes. Families provide labour to each other on a rotational basis. Teams are established for sowing and harvesting and the rich and poor alike share in this communal labour.

Every village has its own artists and craftsmen. So important is their work that the status of villages is determined by the quality of work of its masons, carpenters, metal workers and painters. These products are not for the market, the souvenir trade is supplied from the government crafts shop. Tibetan carpets, *chog-tse* tables (low Tibetan tables) and samovars and Kashmiri handicrafts can be bought in Leh or Kargil. Woolen textiles, particularly Pashmina shawls and tweeds, are also available. Chilling is renowned for its metal craft workers who were originally settlers from Nepal.

In July and August, villagers herd their cattle to the *phu* or high pastures. This is also the time for churning

MUSLIM WOMEN IN NUBRA BAKE NANS OR WHEAT BREAD. THOUGH A SMALL COMMUNITY, NUBRA MUSLIMS ARE A PROSPEROUS AND INFLUENTIAL LOT.

butter, making fuel cakes of animal dung and fermenting *tara*, a popular drink. After harvest, the dzos are taken up to the pasture again, time and weather permitting.

Winter is the time to sit around kitchen fires spinning yarn from raw wool and attending to the animals stabled on the ground floor. These days, families crowd around television sets, since satellite communication has brought modern entertainment to the towns. The carpet loom becomes busy as does the needle stitching new *gonchas* or *jubas*, long gowns favoured by men and women either in rough hand-woven wool or in Chinese velvet.

These days, families are warming their homes with a *shel-khang*, a glass room for passive solar heating, or trombe walls developed by environmentalists from traditional designs using the principle of vacuum heating. Fuel saving is an important cultural practice in the dry desert areas. The *kangri* (a basket with live coal inside a container) from Kashmir is also used to keep oneself warm though it is more fuel intensive.

At first light on a winter morning, large copper trumpets can be heard on the roof top of the monastery, announcing the annual festival. In the courtyard below,

A VIVIDLY PAINTED MURAL COVERING A WALL OF LIKIR *GOMPA* IN LADAKH.

the ritual articles are laid out, while monks dress themselves in robes and masks to participate in the *cham* or masked dances. The large *thang-ka* (religious painting) is unfurled at the entrance. Hemis has an exquisite Chinese *thang-ka*, which is displayed every 12 years. Incense is offered to the *thang-ka* as the music gets louder, reaching a crescendo. The excitement is muted but the anticipation of the main event is palpable. Villagers are free to roam the monastery on festival days offering butter, oil, incense and money to the deities. Merchants set up stalls to tempt villagers and makeshift restaurants provide refreshments.

To the accompaniment of ritual music and chants, the Rimpoche (the head lama who is sometimes a *tulku*, a reincarnate monk) enters the courtyard dressed in his ritual robes. This is a rare sight for many since the Rimpoche is normally busy in meditation and prayers. Villagers who have taken a vow or promised a gift to the monastery on fulfillment of a wish contribute in cash and kind towards holding the festival. The beneficiaries stand before the good and evil spirits, as they perform their ritual battle.

Karsha is an important *gompa* in Zanskar and maintains the classic features of Tibetan feudalism. It holds a substantial part of the land which is tilled by the villagers who bring grain and butter to the monks. Butter is the ultimate gift in this dry and cold land and is the most valuable item in the barter trade. Rangdom is another important *gompa*. It was attacked for its riches by the Bakerwals from Kishtwar in Kashmir at the time of the partition of India.

Each monastery calls its festival by a different name. The festivals of Taktak and Chimrey are known as Anchuk while that of Shey is called Shrulpa. The most famous however are the Chheshu at Hemis monastery and the Dasmochhe at Likir.

The other important festival in the Himalayan region is Losar or the Buddhist New Year which is celebrated at the Palace. King Jamyang advanced the date of Losar as he wanted to invade Skardu on the day of the festival. It is now celebrated on the last two days of the tenth Bodhi month, which falls in December. Houses are illuminated and torchlight processions are taken out through the village. Tampe Chonga, celebrated on the fifteenth day of the first Bodhi month, commemorates Buddha's entry into his mother's womb. Prayers are held at the *gompa* and at home. Jipe Chonga, the fifteenth day of the fourth Bodhi month, is said to be the Buddha's birth anniversary. Devotees fast on this day, offer special prayers and illuminate their homes.

The 'house' is a symbol of family space amongst traditional Buddhists. Earlier, while the father moved out to a shack on the outskirts of the village, the younger son was ordained as a monk and the undivided property was inherited by the eldest son. Since agriculture was dependent on irrigation by small streams, this system worked. The maintenance of the younger brother in the monastery was the responsibility of the elder brother. The family built only one house which anchored all its members and did not put a strain on the environment.

Polygamy was common since a significant proportion of young males were ordained monks.

The elder brother often married all the daughters of a particular family while the rest of the women became nuns.

Even today houses reflect the status of the family. The aristocrats have three-storeyed homes with several wings, each opening on to its own courtyard. Every wing has a prayer room, hall, sitting room, bedroom, dressing room, toilet and a servant's room. On the second floor are the guest rooms and the assembly hall which has a picture of a deity or a Buddhist *acharya*. All festivals and family events are celebrated here. The ground floor houses animals, fodder and the *chang* (strong drink from fermented barley) room. All houses in Tibet face south to catch the sun and this is the general orientation wherever possible.

Many rich families have country estates following the same pattern. Landed families build three-storied houses, the bottom three or four feet of stone, the rest of mud brick, each of which is fairly long. The roofs are flat because of shortage of timber, and covered with willow twigs. This is sufficient protection in the dry climate. Houses do not have chimneys since the heat is required to keep warm in winters. The smoke rises to colour the ceiling with tar. Chrome yellow and red ochre bands are painted below the roof for decoration and poles are put up in the front courtyard, with a yak's tail at the top to ward off the evil eye.

In the Western Himalaya, animals form an important aspect of the family's assets. Self-sufficiency in milk and milk products is essential for survival. The poorer families rely on nomads to provide butter as they can only afford

to keep sheep and goats. Fodder is not plentiful and the animals have to be housed in the winter. Animal heat from the lower floor (the *Tang-ra*) warms the upper floor where the family lives. The winter kitchen (*chensa*) is sometimes located on the leeward side of the lower floor. The summer rooms on the upper floors are much more open and airy. On starry summer nights, youngsters go up to the roof to dream sweet dreams. In winter, the stock of fuel wood is left on the roof which is also used for catching the sun on cold winter mornings.

Today, families have a smokeless *chula*, introduced by the Moravian missionaries. The tin flue helps to clear the room of smoke and the *chensa* is often used as the family room. All houses have a toilet inside and one outside for the use of visitors.

Lahul houses are larger because the extended family system is prevalent here. Younger sons also remain at home and do not join the monastery. While the family house retains its traditional appearance, 'typical' construction favoured by the government in Shimla and Srinagar is changing the face of Kaza, Kyelong and Leh. Houses are located on stilts in the midst of fields greened by mountain streams, or in the labyrinthine town. Atop the hill, facing the village is generally a small votive structure which protects the village from the evil eye.

The Khosias of Kinnaur are Buddhists and live in the areas adjoining Spiti. Polyandry is common amongst the villagers, all the brothers being husbands of the bride. Marriages are restricted to *khandans* or clans which form economic units and are believed to be the regulation of the local deity. Buddhism dominates the Kalpa and Pooh

THE METAL WORKERS OF CHILLING HAVE HANDED DOWN THEIR CRAFT FROM GENERATION TO GENERATION.

districts. Tibetan deities, Tungma and Milayung, are worshipped along with Mahasu Devta and his demonic relations. These are village gods which are approached by the oracle, who determines every decision in the life of the villagers. The village god travels in a palanquin covered with yak's tail. The *yatra* (pilgrimage) around the Kinner Kailash is an important event for these simple and devout people.

Lamaism is practised in Kinnaur. The *gyo-lang* are celibate monks who shave their heads while the *durpus* can marry. *Jamos* or nuns are also seen in large numbers.

They do not have any restrictions on marriage but spend their time reciting the scriptures. Kinners believe that mountain tops, caves and passes are inhabited by supernatural beings, including evil spirits called *khunkch* which are passed on by the sale of animals. *Ban chir*, the ghost of the blue pine, locals say, can assume any shape and cause great damage. Homes are adorned with the horns of domestic animals to ward off these evil spirits.

Pooh and Moorang are alive with festivals throughout the year. Dakhraini, Flaich, Fulaunchi, Sazo and Suskar are celebrated with drinking and merrymaking, although their origins are lost in myth and legend. Dances like Kayang and Bonyungabu are also performed. Wine is offered to the gods and goats are sacrificed as a part of the ritual. Being tribal areas, brewing is a legal activity and the locals make delicious beer from apricots, apples and grapes.

The Lahulas closely resemble the Tibetan and Ladakhi people. Their dialect is also similar. The family forms the basic unit of kinship and as a result of the system of polyandry, the Lahulas follow the system of the extended family. The head is the patriarch, who is the most competent amongst the senior members of the family. He is called the *yundo* and his wife the *yundamo*. Lahulas revere their elders. Families are part of clans or *rhus*. These clans divide the village into units, which then live and work closely. Marriage within the clan is not permitted. However, the mother's family is outside the clan, and this cross-cousin marriage is favoured. The Lahulas are egalitarian and do not discriminate on the basis of caste. They restrict themselves to their own valley. Polyandry has survived into modern times because of the socio-economic poverty of the region and the harsh physical conditions. It has also helped check population pressure on small landholdings. Women are given equal

THE LEH BAZAAR IS WHERE WOMEN SELL VEGETABLES, GOSSIP AND REFRESH THEMSELVES WITH *CHANG* OR BARLEY BEER (SEE THE WHITE BOTTLE).

status in society. Divorce is not common but when it occurs, the husband has to pay compensation to the woman if she does not remarry.

Hinduism and Buddhism are closely linked in Lahul. At the temple of Trilokinath in Tandi, the same image is worshipped by the Hindus as Shiva and by the Buddhists as Avilokateshwara. Pilgrims from Spiti and Ladakh also come to worship here. Halda or Losar is a popular festival. Celebrated in January, it is akin to Diwali, the Hindu festival of lamps. Siskar Apa, the goddess of wealth in the Buddhist pantheon, is worshipped like Lakshmi, her Hindu counterpart. Torchlight processions are taken out through towns and villages and all the people meet at a spot determined by the lamas, where a bonfire is lit. Drinking, feasting and dancing are the secular part of the ritual.

Spiti is a Buddhist stronghold. The monasteries control daily life and some of the most important monasteries are located here. In 1996, Tabo monastery celebrated its thousand year anniversary. People from all over the country came to worship, led by the Dalai Lama. Said to be one of the 108 monasteries constructed by the great translator, Rinchin-Tsang-po in his propagation of the Buddhist faith in the Himalaya, Tabo is renowned all through the world. It is not on the crown of a hill and its mud-plastered walls merge into the countryside. Inside, in the dark halls, life-size images mounted on high platforms surround the visitors. Miniature panels, including the famous 1,000 Buddhas, can be seen on the walls.

Bumkhor is another important festival when religious books are carried around the fields. The procession is lead by a lama who chants *mantras* to ensure a plentiful harvest. The villagers gather around to offer prayers, food and *chang*.

The Ladarch and Pori fairs are well-attended by the farming community as well as the nomads. People dress in the particular style of their valley and the dances also reflect the costumes and masks of the region. The Chandra, the Bhaga and the Chenab valleys have their own fairs and festivals, since each area has subsisted through these interlinks. However, the mobility of the people has had cross-cultural influences in all the valleys.

The Muslim and Christian communities that have become a part of the Buddhist world celebrate their own festivals like Id and Christmas, but the folk form of celebration gathers all the communities together in a bond of fun and frolic.

To our city-bred, 'scientific' minds, the common fears of the people and their popular imagination, their traditional medical systems (the inspiration for *ayurveda*), rituals and taboos may seem quaint, archaic, exotic or simply out-of-date. However, Buddhism has an integral spirituality, a holistic world within which it seems plausible to live one's life according to the wisdom of the lamas and the regulations of the ancestors, who have created a sustainable world where others have feared to tread.

FOLLOWING PAGE: THE LANDSCAPE OF MUSTANG IS A BARREN MOONSCAPE OF ERODED SANDSTONE PILLARS AND DISCONTINUOUS MORAINE TERRACES, WHICH TOGETHER PRESENT A COLORFUL MOSAIC MADE UP PRINCIPALLY OF EARTHEN REDS, YELLOWS AND BROWN.

Mustang:
The Land Of
Peace And
Frugality

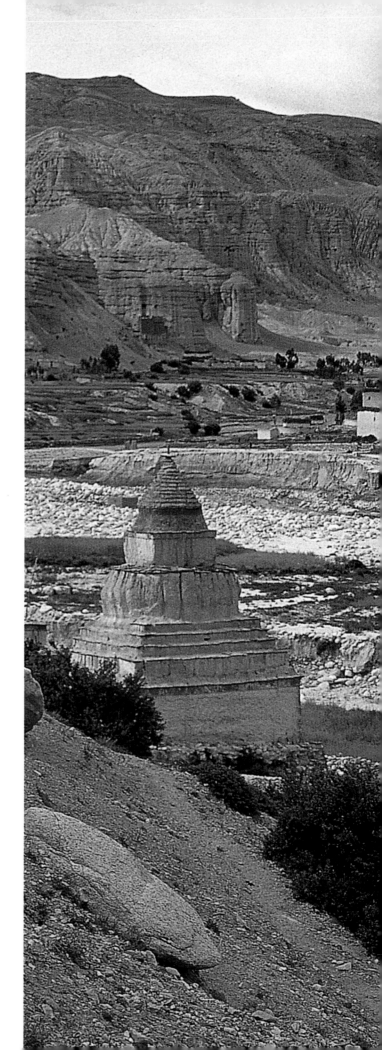

The Kali Gandhak valley in Mustang, Nepal is perhaps the most dramatic region in the Himalaya. The river pierces the Dhaulagiri and Annapurna ranges and one can actually see evidence of the great thrust fault that is said to have given such immense height to the Himalaya. As one climbs the valley, the humid and sub-tropical weather gives way to the cold and the arid. Along with the climatic change, there is also a transformation in the cultural and agricultural practices.

The dry cold winds that blow from the Tibetan plateau rush through this valley whose walls rise to over 5,000 meters. Jomosom, the entrance to the Mustang valley, is thus subjected to swirling, blustery dust storms made more intense due to the surface conditions. In the bygone days, this was the traditional route to Tibet. As one travels from Jomosom to Thanti, the valley widens out and one can see Tukche set in the dusty, arid landscape, like a speck of sand below an azure sky; the land mass pushing into the heart of Asia. Amonite fragments and fossils in the rock add a black outline to the sun-dazed eyes. This region is known as Thak Khola, after the Thakals who have peopled this natural corridor to give economic and cultural access to the landlocked Tibetan plateau.

This corridor is a path for pilgrims as well as for nature-lovers. The Tibeto-Nepalese tribes who have made their home here are mainly Sherpas and Thakals. They speak a Tibetan dialect and follow the lamaist tradition of

THE WINDSWEPT PLAIN OF MUSTANG AT AN INCREDIBLE
HEIGHT OF 12,400 FEET.

Buddhism. Their two-storeyed houses, *chang* and *tsampa* meals and their art of story-telling are reminiscent of the simplicity of the old way of life. Khamba tribes from Tibet have also settled in the Mustang valley, after the flight of the Dalai Lama from Tibet.

From Muktinath, where the temple of Jwala Mai has a natural flame burning constantly, pilgrims take the route to the Kali Gandhak valley. Called the Black River, the Krishna Gandaki rises in a lake on the Tibetan plateau and flows down to the Ganges. This is an important trade route in the Himalaya. Thakal traders control this trade link, their pack animals loaded with salt. They survive on *rakshi*, a strong brew of rice and millet. This route is, however, misused by the Khambas for smuggling rare and valuable artifacts from Tibet.

Tukche is the main resting point between the two mountain ranges. The valley floor is flat with incredibly steep walls of rock rising on all sides. The dust bowl of the Himalaya lies just beyond this insignificant outpost. At night, as the light flickers in the cold wind, stories of Yeti are common around camp fires. A mythical beast, the Yeti is either an ape or a bear which lost its natural habitat when the Himalaya rose. The locals believe that whoever sees it will be possessed by evil spirits. Yeti lore goes beyond mere footprints, it includes the stealing of yak and kidnapping of young girls.

The pass at Nisango is a 15,000 ft wall of red earth beyond which the desert flourishes. Virtually treeless, the villagers in this region have a hard life. They trek for days looking for fuel wood. The winter is so bitterly cold that it is difficult to keep warm.

Mustang is a remote enclave of western Nepal. Its capital, Lo Manthang lies at a height of 12,400 ft on a windswept plain, far from any road leading to the modern world. Its small community of herdsmen leave their white-washed homes early to reach the pastures. Some who own land go past the walls of the town to the terraced fields. The rest of the region is a desert of scree and dirt, an expanse of gorges and cliffs, where every drop of water is treasured. Till recently, Mustang was closed to outsiders because it became a launching pad for Tibetan resistance. Closure led to the severance of its traditional ties with Tibet. The monks from the monasteries in Mustang now study in Nepal or India but this has diluted the rural culture of the people.

As in the rest of the Himalaya, in Mustang too, the traditional power of the king has been undermined by the police, bureaucrats and teachers of the government. The 600 year old tradition of Mustang is best illustrated by its Tiji festival, a spring rite. The copper horns herald the beginning of the festival as the abbot, dressed in ceremonial robes, emerges from the gate of the walled capital town. Five monks follow behind, carrying bowls of water containing evil spirits. The spirits are believed have been captured in the three days of dancing and singing that preceded the beginning of the cleansing rites. The king, adorned in a golden robe with a turquoise ear-ring—that symbolises membership to the court of the Dalai Lamas—fires his gun in the air. The joyous crowds from distant villages watch the bowls being dashed to the ground one by one, symbolising the destruction of the forces of

PRAYER FLAGS FLUTTERING OVER THE YANGSHA REFUGEE CAMP. THE RED STRUCTURE ON THE FAR LEFT IS THE YANGSHA *GOMPA*.

fire, flood, drought, famine and earthquake. As the crowds return to the village, they jump over the ceremonial fire lit at the gate so that the bad spirits do not re-enter the village.

The abbot of the monastery, a lama since he was eleven years old, explains that the Tiji is a rite of peace that encompasses all faiths. Tourism has undermined its sacred significance and most people view it as a spectacle, a touch of local colour or a remnant of the past. As the *thang-ka* of the Vairocana Buddha is unfurled, the entertainment value overshadows the ancient rite of asking for blessings. Today, an airstrip has been constructed at Jomosom, but it is still a nine-day trek to Lo Manthang at the top of the valley, located between the ancient monasteries of Luri to the south and Chudzong to the north. Village houses are adorned with 'spirit catchers'.

The ancient trade of grain and salt has been replaced by trading sweaters from Punjab and Assam. This has helped those who have remained behind to buy articles of daily use from the market. The attractions of the southern valleys include the excitement of watching Indian movies

THE FEARSOME TANTRIC IMAGE OF MAHAKALA IN
MUSTANG, NEPAL.

on the video and carrying back posters to decorate their mud walls. The four-storey high palace approached by a wooden staircase and guarded by a prayer wheel is an impressive structure. Hierarchy still survives in Mustang. No one can sit on a platform higher than that of the king, the descendent of Ame Pal who united the warring tribes in 1380. There is also a caste system. Butchers and blacksmiths are considered unclean and therefore forbidden entry into the house. The poverty of the people and intrusion of the central government in civic affairs have undermined the culture. The ecological and cultural fragility of Mustang is further endangered by the entry of tourists. Two decades have brought greater changes than the hundreds of years that have gone by.

At its peak, the rulers of Mustang patronised art and scholarship that all Buddhist kingdoms in the Western Himalaya are known for. The 40 ft high gilded statue of the Maitreya Buddha in the Jampa temple at Lo Manthang is a living reminder of the cultural heights that the artists of Mustang had achieved. *Mane* walls and *chortens* guard the walls of the villages in the valley. Ornately-bound scriptural texts are found in the wayside monasteries. Temples and *gompas* hum with the sound of Buddhist chanting. However, the independent kingdom of Mustang ceased to exist when it was incorporated into the Kingdom of Nepal in the eighteenth century. Since then, the Buddhist heritage is in decay, people have neither the time nor the money for its survival.

Agricultural practices remain traditional. In the post-summer harvest, wheat is winnowed with cries to the wind to take away the chaff. A good harvest is the resullt

VILLAGES CLUSTER NEAR THE RIVER, FORMING AN OASIS. THE OCHRE WALLS INDICATE A MONASTERY.

of not only the hard work of the farmer and his yak, but the successful driving away of demons during Tiji. The grain is stored in sacks made from yaks' hair; and dung is collected in baskets to make cakes for the winter ahead.

As one leaves the village, the parting rite is performed. Lung-ta Tang-en involves lighting a fire with juniper wood and incense. As the fire burns, scraps of cloth on which prayers have been written are thrown to the wind that howls through the gorge. As in other parts of the Himalaya, the prayers express the hope that the visitor may return home safely.

As stubborn as the yak which can survive the thin air and on meagre forage, the farmers of Mustang are a hardy lot. Their barter system includes dried yak dung exchanged for the farmer's grain. Herdsmen come down from their tented world, their goatskin bags full of yak butter. With this money, they shop in the market or buy household utensils on the trade route. The sight of the terraced fields greened by narrow irrigation channels must be welcome after the long trek through frost-hardened mountains. Milking closely bunched goats and bringing to life fields of grain, the herders and farmers tend their resources with great care. How long this caution will last, with the new trends from the plains coming in, remains to be seen. At the moment Mustang remains a hidden corner, a lost world, a caravan *serai*.

As our journey through the Himalayan Desert comes to an end, the universal spirit of love and compassion that permeates the high valleys, the mud-walled villages and the meditative peace of the *gompas* lives on.

A TRAVELLER CROSSES THE ROPE BRIDGE, OVER THE ZANSKAR RIVER IN LADAKH.

DOLPA in the western region of Nepal has been rarely visited because it adjoins areas which have been designated as restricted. However, its scenic beauty and historical importance are as rich as the Kathmandu or Pokhra valleys. Bordering Tibet, this valley is enclosed by a ring of massive mountains which kept it culturally and environmentally secure. Dolpa became a part of Nepal 200 years ago when the Gorkhas gained control. But its cultural life remains closely linked to Tibetan Buddhism even today.

Shey and Ban-Thang are the principal valleys where the sparse population of Rangbar, the 'valley farmers' and the Drok, nomadic herdsmen, eke out a living at elevations beyond 4,000 meters. Air services are available to Jamla, the fourteenth century capital of the Khasa Mallas who controlled the area from Taklakhar in western Tibet to the Terai. The town has several fine temples which are proof of its golden past. However, the flights are not very frequent and food and accommodation is extremely basic.

Dolpa closely resembles Ladakh and Spiti with high winds swirling around the village before noon. North of the valley is the Shey Phoksumdo National Park. Established in 1981, it is Nepal's biggest national park and straddles the Dolpa and Mugu districts and extends across the Kanji Roba Himal to the Tibetan border. This region has peaks over 6,000 meters in height and a variety of environments ranging from that of the lower Himalaya to the arid vastness of the southern Tibetan plateau. Animals, which have adapted to the high cold desert

A DOLPA GIRL PEEPING OUT OF HER WINDOW.

LEFT: HEMMED IN BY STEEP MOUNTAINS LIES THE DOLPA VALLEY IN WESTERN NEPAL.

climate, like the gazelle and the wild yak thrive here. But the pride of the region is of course the snow leopard, an endangered species found commonly at high attitudes in the mountain ranges that surround Central Asia. The main attractions of the park are the lake and the 1,000 year old Shey *gompa* which attract pilgrims from all over the Dolpa district. Its principal festival takes place on the Purnima (full moon) day in August every year when pilgrims circumambulate the Shey mountain on three consecutive days. From Phoksumdo, we follow the river to the village of Pungmi and towards the lush meadows to view the spectacular Kajmera peaks.

These relatively isolated villages are peopled by a variety of ethnic groups who have evolved a distinct culture. Their dances are extremely liberal and include the *Ghatu* which is performed by young virgins on Buddha Purnima day (the Buddha's birthday). This dance is influenced by Tantricism as the dancers fall into a trance during the performance. Village houses painted in yellow indicate the wealth of the monks while those washed in white belong to the lay population. This region is extremely difficult to enter since there are no roads and much of the trekking is over 3,000 meters high.

SNOWFIELD AND BHAGA
RIVER IN LAHUL.

PHOTO
CREDITS

SPITI: KAZA, TABO AND PIN FORM A TRIANGLE WHICH IS THE CORE AREA OF INTEREST AND
HABITATION. THANGYUD *GOMPA* IN SPITI.